D1279052

Barry C. Parsons

Rock Recipes

The *Best* Food From My Newfoundland Kitchen

WWW.BREAKWATERBOOKS.COM

Breakwater Books is committed to choosing papers and materials for our books that help to protect our environment. To this end, this book is printed on a recycled paper that is certified by the Forest Stewardship Council of Canada.

LIBRARY AND ARCHIVES CANADA CATALOGUING IN PUBLICATION
Parsons, Barry C., author
Rock recipes : the best food from my Newfoundland kitchen / Barry C. Parsons.
Includes index.
ISBN 978-1-55081-555-9 (bound)
1. Cooking, Canadian--Newfoundland and Labrador style.
2. Cooking--Newfoundland and Labrador. 3. Cookbooks I. Title.
TX715.6.P367 2014   641.59718   C2014-901925-4

Copyright © 2014 Barry C. Parsons

All Rights Reserved. No part of this work covered by the copyright hereon may be reproduced or used in any form or by any means–graphic, electronic or mechanical–without the prior written permission of the publisher. Any request for photocopying, recording, taping or storing in an information retrieval system of any part of this book shall be directed in writing to Access Copyright, One Yonge Street, Suite 800, Toronto, Ontario, M5E 1E5.

Canada

Newfoundland
Labrador

We acknowledge the financial support of the Government of Canada through the Canada Book Fund (CBF) and the Government of Newfoundland and Labrador through the Department of Tourism, Culture and Recreation for our publishing activities.

PRINTED AND BOUND IN CANADA.
Reprinted 2015, 2016

To Barry
H. Ruby

Christmas 1980

For

Ruby Yetman, who thought a Betty Crocker Cookbook was
a perfectly fine Christmas gift for a fifteen-year-old boy.

Contents

"I was a curious kid in their kitchens."

Let's get one thing out of the way from the very beginning:
I am not a chef.

I've never taken a cooking lesson in my life, except from my mom, grandmothers, or aunts when I was a curious kid in their kitchens. I'm just an enthusiastic home cook who's had a lifelong love of cooking, baking, and developing my own recipes by experimenting in the kitchen. My culinary experiments started even before my teen years with a particular love of baking, and from there, advanced into cooking as well. I was quite a finicky eater as a child, and I think I subconsciously learned that if I cooked, I controlled what went on the dinner table for my parents and five siblings. I still tell parents of picky eaters today not to be too hard on their discerning kids; they might all turn out to be pretty good cooks one day.

With years of cooking and baking experience under my belt, like many others with plenty of kitchen know-how, I've developed a pretty good sense of what ingredients will work well together in a main dish and what flavors, textures, and ingredient proportions work well in a good baking recipe too. That means my kitchen adventures these days are much more hits than the sometimes misses of my trial-and-error early days. I always say I am my own best teacher but also my most inefficient.

I don't have a sprawling gourmet kitchen. I have a 10' x 11' kitchen with not nearly enough counter space. I've never paid thousands, or even hundreds, for a set of high-end cookware or bake ware. I don't have all the latest gadgets or much interest in them either. Other than my stove, the most expensive thing in my kitchen is my Kitchen Aid stand mixer. A food processor and a blender are my only two other small kitchen appliances. My point, of course, is that it's the cook that makes the meal and not the cooking implements. I tell young cooks starting out to learn about cooking basics first and decide what their kitchens actually need as they hone their skills and learn more. Some of us would have saved a fortune with that approach.

My food philosophy is pretty simple: Real quality ingredients and a good simple recipe is all it takes to prepare real everyday food for real people. I was once in a supermarket line where the lady behind me was struggling to keep masses of cardboard and plastic over-packaged products from spilling out of two overloaded carts. My one cart was full of ingredients to actually cook meals with...plus I probably had twice the food as her at half the cost. While many of the popular recipes on my blog and in these pages can sometimes be a little indulgent, I contend that if you are not eating out of packages, you are still eating better than many. I say balanced eating is much more achievable with real food than with preservative ridden processed foods.

This book is a collection of some of the most popular recipes on my *Rock Recipes* blog, gathered over the past seven years, with a few of my personal favorites and some brand new recipes developed just for this book too. The recipes have been tried successfully by thousands of real people who, probably just like you, are simply trying to get dinner on the table each weeknight, who like an occasional slow-cooked Sunday comfort-food meal, and who maybe even enjoy finding the perfect celebration cake or dessert to share with family and friends. My purpose in writing this book is to present achievable recipes that anyone will have success with, from an absolute beginner home cook to one with years of experience looking for more great useable recipes. I get amazing positive feedback from folks who follow my blog and regularly try my recipes; it's one of the most gratifying things about sharing them over the past several years.

And I am definitely not a pro photographer. I've always had a philosophy that you can teach yourself practically anything if you have the time. The limited amount that I know about taking a decent photo definitely comes from that trial-and-error mentality. I bought my first decent camera in order to take plenty of baby photos when my daughter was born, and other than reading a beginner photography book to get the basics, I've never had a lesson in that either.

There's no doubt that the photos on *Rock Recipes* have gotten better over the years, and I have re-shot some of the older ones for this book, but I still see the pictures mainly as illustrations for the recipes, to give an indication of what the finished product should look like. They're shot as fuss-free as possible and almost always in natural window light with only a simple reflector as an aid. The photos for these recipes aren't elaborately staged; truth be told, the vast majority of photos on my blog were shot in photo sessions of under five minutes, just before the food goes on the table to eat. I said in one interview a while back that my primary photo-shooting rule is, "Don't let it get cold, it's dinner!" It sounds like a joke, but it's quite near the truth in most of my food photos.

My hope is that you'll find this book practical and useful. I hope it can make weekday dinners easier, slow-cooked Sundays more relaxing, and celebrations with family and friends more delicious. I hope it provides a little inspiration to beginner cooks, maybe a few new go-to recipes for seasoned cooks, and maybe a pinch of encouragement for everyone to try their own twists on any of my recipes. I've always said that a good recipe is always just a good starting point; it's up to you to make the dish your own.

If there's one thing I've learned from the last seven years of blogging it's you can't possibly post too many great chicken recipes. Right from the beginning, chicken recipes have been our most searched and most popular recipes. In fact, four out of the top ten recipes ever on *Rock Recipes* are chicken dishes. It seems folks are constantly looking for delicious ways to serve up this key dinnertime ingredient.

There are well over a hundred chicken recipes posted on my blog, and those included in this book represent some of the most popular and provide quite a good cross section of the types of recipes I've featured. From an incredibly popular honey garlic chicken recipe to Greek, Indian, and Asian inspired selections, plus a couple of healthier option recipes, there's plenty of inspiration in this collection to answer the perennial question of how to make something new from this most popular dinner staple.

Main Dishes: Chicken

Double Crunch Honey Garlic Chicken Breasts

SERVES 4

4 large boneless skinless chicken breasts

2 cups flour

4 tsp salt

4 tsp black pepper

3 tbsp ground ginger

1 tbsp freshly ground nutmeg

2 tsp ground thyme

2 tsp ground sage

2 tbsp paprika

1 tsp cayenne pepper

4 eggs + 8 tbsp water, whisked to make an egg wash

canola oil for frying

HONEY GARLIC SAUCE

2 tbsp olive oil

3-4 cloves garlic, minced

1 cup honey

¼ cup soy sauce (low-sodium soy sauce is best)

1 tsp ground black pepper

Do these chicken breasts look good or what? This recipe has been among the most commented on and the most raved about dishes I've ever posted, and for very good reason. Everyone who tries them loves them and makes them over and over again. So many readers have sent thanks for this recipe and shared it with their friends, declaring it's become a new favourite in their family and a permanent fixture in their dinner planning menus.

Because the chicken breasts are pounded out to a ½-inch thickness, they fry very quickly while still providing a juicy interior and a super crunchy exterior, a big reason for this recipe's popularity. A quick dip in the easily prepared honey garlic sauce adds a sweet and slightly salty finish that everyone just loves. I serve mine with some thin Chinese egg noodles, lightly tossed in the same sauce, and a few sautéed vegetables on the side. Workday dinners just don't get better than this.

1.   Place the chicken breasts between 2 sheets of plastic wrap and using a meat mallet, pound the meat to an even ½-inch thickness. Alternatively, you can slice the breasts by placing them flat on a cutting board and using a very sharp knife to slice them into halves horizontally.

2.   Sift together the flour, salt, black pepper, ground ginger, nutmeg, thyme, sage, paprika, and cayenne pepper. NOTE: This flour and spice dredge mix is sufficient for two batches of this chicken recipe. Store half of the mix in a Ziploc bag in the freezer for the next time you make this recipe...and there will be a next time.

3.   Make an egg wash by whisking together the eggs and water.

4. Season the chicken breasts with salt and pepper then dip the meat in the flour and spice mixture. Dip the breast into the egg wash and then a final time in the flour and spice mix, pressing the mix into the meat to get good contact.

5. Heat a skillet on the stove with about a ½-inch of canola oil covering the bottom. You will want to carefully regulate the temperature here so the chicken does not brown too quickly. The thinness of the breast meat practically guarantees it will be fully cooked by the time the outside is browned. I find just below medium heat works well. I use a burner setting of about 4½ out of 10 on the dial and fry them gently for about 4-5 minutes per side until golden brown and crispy.

6. Drain on a wire rack for a couple of minutes before dipping the cooked breasts into the Honey Garlic Sauce. Serve with noodles or rice.

HONEY GARLIC SAUCE

1. In a medium saucepan add 2 tbsp olive oil and the minced garlic. Cook over medium heat to soften the garlic but do not let it brown.

2. Add the honey, soy sauce, and black pepper.

3. Simmer together for 5-10 minutes, remove from heat, and allow to cool for a few minutes. Watch this carefully as it simmers because it can foam up over the pot very easily.

Honey Soy
Chicken Breasts

SERVES **4**

4 large chicken breasts
(not boneless, skinless)

MARINADE

¼ cup honey

⅓ cup light soy sauce

½ tsp freshly ground
black pepper

4 cloves garlic, minced

1 tbsp finely grated fresh ginger
root

In just a few minutes, you can prepare this 5 ingredient marinade in the morning or the previous evening to have this chicken ready to pop into the oven when you arrive home from work. About 45 minutes open roasting time is all these golden, sticky chicken breasts need; more than enough time to throw together a great salad, steam rice, or prepare your favourite noodles. If serving with noodles or rice, I recommend doubling the marinade/sauce recipe.

1. Stir together all the marinade ingredients and pour into a large Ziploc bag. Add the chicken breasts and marinate in the fridge for a couple of hours or overnight.

2. Preheat oven to 375°F. Place the marinated chicken breasts on an aluminum foil-lined cookie sheet and bake, uncovered, for about 45 minutes or until the chicken is fully cooked. I use a meat thermometer to make sure the internal temperature is between 170°-180°F.

3. Do not throw out the marinade. While the chicken is cooking, simmer it over low heat and brush it on the chicken about every 10 minutes as it cooks.

Chicken Souvlaki
with Lemon Mint Tzatziki

SERVES **4**

SOUVLAKI MARINADE

6 tbsp fresh lemon juice

3 tbsp olive oil

2 tbsp balsamic vinegar

½ tsp kosher salt

1 rounded tbsp smoked paprika

1 tsp freshly ground black pepper

3 cloves garlic, minced

4 large boneless skinless chicken breasts

4 long bamboo skewers

bell pepper or red onion

LEMON MINT TZATZIKI

3 cups Greek yogurt, drained

6-inch piece of English cucumber

1 tsp kosher salt

2 tbsp finely chopped fresh mint

2 cloves garlic, minced

3 tbsp fresh lemon juice

2 tbsp olive oil

pinch of salt and pepper

Greek food is a family favourite at our house, and this simple but very flavourful dish is yet another way to pull a great meal off the summertime grill or even using your broiler. This particular souvlaki and tzatziki is a personal favourite that I regularly crave, and goes well with a Greek salad or flatbread.

The chicken need only be marinated for 15-20 minutes to infuse it with intense lemon-garlic flavour. My souvlaki marinade also uses a small splash of balsamic vinegar and some smoked paprika for extra layers of flavour. This marinade also works very well with pork tenderloin or lamb, which can be marinated much longer than chicken if you prefer.

There are a couple of herbs that work well in a good tzatziki, including parsley or dill, but my absolute favourite is finely chopped fresh mint that I pluck from a small herb bed in the garden, just a few feet from the kitchen door. Working against the tangy zing of lemon and Greek yogurt, I like the balancing freshness that mint brings to this bright accompaniment to a great souvlaki. It also makes a fantastic dressing for Greek salad or as a veggie dip.

> tip > I like to pound out the chicken breasts to about ¼-inch thickness to provide as much surface space as possible to accept the marinade and increase the flavour. I then cut the thin marinated chicken into about 1x3-inch pieces and fold them over before piercing the meat.

suggestion > Serve with a Greek salad, flatbread, and tzatziki.

SOUVLAKI MARINADE

1. Mix the first 7 ingredients together and pour over the chicken in a Ziploc bag. Toss the chicken around well in the marinade to coat on all sides. Marinate in the fridge for 15-20 minutes. While the chicken is marinating, soak 4 long bamboo skewers in water. Pierce the chicken onto the skewers, alternating with pieces of bell pepper or red onion. Cook on a preheated grill at medium-high heat for about 6 minutes before turning over and grilling for an additional 6 minutes on the opposite side or until the chicken is completely cooked through.

LEMON MINT TZATZIKI

1. Draining the yogurt removes much of the liquid and produces an end product about the consistency of thick sour cream. To drain the yogurt, line a colander with several layers of cheesecloth (or in a pinch, several large coffee filters). Pour the yogurt into the colander and place it over a large bowl in the fridge for a couple of hours. This should produce about 2 cups of thick yogurt.

2. Peel the piece of cucumber and remove the seeds and pulp at the center with a teaspoon. Then dice the outside flesh of the cucumber into small cubes of ⅛-inch or less.

3. Sprinkle 1 teaspoon of kosher salt over the diced cucumber, and toss together well. Let this rest for about 30 minutes, stirring occasionally. This process removes some of the liquid from the cucumber, so it will not water down the consistency of your finished tzatziki. Drain all the liquid off the diced cucumber before adding it to the drained yogurt along with the fresh mint, minced garlic, lemon juice, olive oil, salt, and pepper.

4. Mix well, cover, and store in the fridge for at least 30 minutes before serving.

Honey Dijon Glazed Chicken Breasts

SERVES 4

4 large chicken breasts (not boneless, skinless)

⅓ cup + ¼ cup honey

½ tsp freshly ground black pepper

3 cloves garlic, minced

¼ cup Dijon mustard

3 tbsp lemon juice

1 tbsp light soy sauce

Another of the most popular chicken recipes ever on *Rock Recipes*, this one's very easy and very delicious with a wonderful sweet and savory sticky glaze in the classic combination of honey with Dijon mustard.

1. Stir together ⅓ cup honey with the pepper, garlic, Dijon mustard, lemon juice, and soy sauce. Pour over the chicken breasts in a large Ziploc bag and marinate in the fridge for at least a couple of hours.

2. Preheat oven to 375°F. Place the marinated chicken breasts on an aluminum foil-lined cookie sheet and bake, uncovered, for about 45 minutes or until the chicken is fully cooked. I use a meat thermometer to make sure the internal temperature is between 170° and 180°F.

3. Do not throw out the marinade. Instead, add the additional ¼ cup of honey, and while the chicken is cooking, simmer the marinade over low heat and brush it repeatedly on the chicken during the last 30 minutes of cooking time; about every 10 minutes as it cooks.

Easy Broiled Lemon Chicken

This is my kind of recipe: quick, easy, and super tasty. It seems nobody broils anything anymore, but this recipe has taught me that it may be a grossly under-used cooking method. I first saw a similar recipe idea on a TV show and was struck by the short cooking time as well as the quick and easy preparation. I do recommend using a meat thermometer to get the cooking time exactly right, but when you do, this chicken turns out succulent and juicy with plenty of lemon infused flavour.

In terms of the amount of effort involved to achieve the level of flavour that results, I would probably have to call this the best lemon chicken recipe I've ever tried. Broiling the chicken also provides some very tasty pan drippings. I skim the excess fat and pour the drippings into a gravy boat to serve with the chicken.

SERVES 4–6

1 whole **chicken**, cut in pieces (or about 3 lbs chicken pieces)

3 tbsp **olive oil**

½ tsp **salt**

½ tsp **freshly ground black pepper**

1 tsp **dried oregano**

juice of 2 large or **3 small lemons** (reserve the peels for the roasting pan)

1. Wash your chicken pieces well and pat dry with paper towels. Add the chicken pieces to a large shallow pan. It is very important not to crowd the chicken pieces in the pan. They should not touch each other at all and should have at least a ½-inch of space between the pieces for good heat circulation and even browning. If necessary, use two smaller pans in order not to crowd the pieces together. To the pan add the olive oil, salt, black pepper, oregano, and lemon juice.

2. Toss together well then massage the chicken pieces with the lemon, oil, and seasonings. Spread out the pieces in the pan. Add the lemon peel pieces to the pan as well; the roasted lemon pieces add extra flavour to the pan drippings.

3. Because individual broilers vary greatly, you will have to use some judgement in the cooking method and time to suit your individual broiler. I broiled this chicken on high but kept the pan on the second lowest rack from the bottom. Watch the chicken carefully so it does not brown too quickly. If it does start to brown too quickly, lower the rack even further, or if possible, turn the temperature down on your broiler. If your broiler is temperature controlled, I would set it at about 400° to 425°F.

4. It's important to turn the chicken several times during the broiling time. I turned the pieces about 4 times during the 35-40 minute cooking time. Use a meat thermometer to take a reading from the center of the largest pieces of chicken, and when the internal temperature reaches 170°F, remove the pieces from the oven and let rest for 5 minutes before serving. Skim the excess fat from the pan drippings and serve with the chicken.

Oven Fried Chicken

SERVES 4-6

3 lbs chicken pieces

3 cups flour

1 tbsp salt

1 tbsp freshly ground black pepper

2 tbsp onion powder

1 tbsp garlic powder

1 tbsp powered thyme

1 tbsp powered sage

1 tbsp dried basil

1 tbsp dried oregano

1 tbsp dried marjoram

1 tbsp dry mustard powder

1 tbsp powdered ginger

1 tbsp paprika

1 tbsp cayenne pepper

2 eggs + 2 tbsp water, whisked to make an egg wash

canola oil

My Oven Fried Chicken recipe is really just my standard fried chicken recipe in a simplified, fuss-free, and lighter version. I make the seasoning mixture in large batches and keep it in the freezer in airtight containers to reuse for later. Very little of it goes to waste at our house because we use it for chicken nuggets for the kids, fried chicken fillet sandwiches, and of course good old fried chicken.

1. Combine flour, salt, black pepper, onion powder, garlic powder, thyme, sage, basil, oregano, marjoram, mustard powder, ginger, paprika, and cayenne pepper.

2. Cut one whole chicken into parts or use 3 lbs chicken parts of your choice. Dip the chicken pieces in egg wash of 2 eggs beaten together with 2 tbsp water then dredge thoroughly in the flour and spice mixture to coat the pieces evenly.

3. Coat the bottom of a cookie sheet or large baking pan with the canola oil (light olive oil or peanut oil are also good).

4. Preheat the oven to 375°F. Place the coated chicken pieces in the pan and lightly spray the tops with canola oil from a spray bottle. Bake in the preheated oven for 50-60 minutes, depending on the size of the chicken pieces. I use a meat thermometer to make sure the internal temperature of the largest pieces reaches 170°F.

Quick and Easy Butter Chicken

SERVES 4-6

8 large boneless skinless **chicken thighs**, cut into bite-sized pieces

3 tbsp **butter**

3 tbsp **peanut oil**

3+4 tsp **garam masala**

salt and **pepper** to season

6+1 **cloves garlic**, minced

1 large **white onion**, diced

6 large **ripe tomatoes**, diced

4 **seeded green chilies**, chopped (if green chilies are not available, substitute crushed red chili paste or cayenne pepper to taste)

½ cup **plain, unsweetened yogurt**

1 tsp **ground cardamom**

1 tsp **freshly ground nutmeg**

1 tsp **ground cumin**

2 tbsp **chili powder**

2 tbsp **lemon juice**

4 tbsp finely grated **fresh ginger**

¼ cup melted **butter**

1 cup **chicken stock**

2 tbsp **honey** (more or less to taste)

½ cup **cream**

If you're looking for the definitive recipe for butter chicken, keep looking and good luck. There are many, many different recipe versions out there, geared to many different tastes.

My own recipe is one suited to my own taste and is really a dish created by cherry-picking the best of several recipes I've tried or read. Some recipes do not include cardamom, for example, which has become an essential spice in my version. The bottom line is that, like many dishes I cook, I use a good recipe as a starting point from which I add to or subtract from to suit my own taste. I encourage anyone to do the same.

> **tip** > When purchasing chicken thighs, it's best to buy them already deboned with the skin removed. In my tests, over half of the overall package weight was comprised of skin and bones. This means that even at double the price, the boneless skinless thighs are probably still a better value, and you save yourself all the extra work too.

1. I use boneless skinless chicken thighs in this recipe, which I cut into bite-sized pieces because it's faster than using whole chicken pieces and because I like to simmer the chicken in the sauce for a while before serving. You can use chicken breast pieces if you like, but simmering chicken breast for any length of time will dry it out considerably, so you may just want to add it back to the sauce for only a minute or two to reheat before serving.

2. The chicken for this recipe can simply be sautéed as in the recipe, but when I have access to the backyard grill, I like to grill it for extra smoky flavour.

3. To a large, covered Dutch oven over medium heat add the 3 tbsp butter and peanut oil. Season the chicken thighs with salt and pepper as well as the 3 tsp of garam masala. Add to the pot and brown the pieces for 4-5 minutes. Remove chicken from pan and set aside. Add 6 cloves of minced garlic and the diced white onion.

4. Sauté the onions and garlic in the butter and oil until softened. Increase the heat to medium-high and add the diced tomatoes.

5. Sauté the tomatoes until they break down and form a chunky sauce. Add the sautéed tomatoes and onions to a large blender or food processor along with the chopped green chilies, yogurt, 4 tsp garam masala, cardamom, nutmeg, cumin, chili powder, lemon juice, ginger, 1 clove minced garlic, and ¼ cup melted butter.

6. Puree all ingredients together and return to the pot along with the chicken stock. Simmer together until the sauce is reduced in volume by about ¼.

7. Add the chicken back to the pot and simmer slowly for 10-15 minutes. Finish the dish by adding the honey (more or less to taste) and cream.

8. Simmer for an additional minute or two before serving over rice or with naan.

Phyllo Chicken Prosciutto Margherita

SERVES 4

PHYLLO CHICKEN PROSCIUTTO MARGHERITA

4 large boneless chicken breasts

salt and pepper to season

2 cloves garlic, minced

1 pkg frozen phyllo pastry, thawed

1 cup melted butter

8 thin slices prosciutto

fresh basil leaves

6 oz fresh mozzarella

ROASTED FENNEL AND TOMATO SAUCE

8 large ripe tomatoes, diced

1 large fennel bulb, diced

1 medium red onion, diced

4 cloves garlic, chopped

4 tbsp olive oil

2 tbsp brown sugar

½ tsp crushed chillies (optional)

salt and pepper to taste

2 tbsp fresh oregano, chopped

2 tbsp chives, chopped

3 tbsp balsamic vinegar

An ideal dinner party idea that can be prepared in advance and popped into the oven when drinks and nibbles are served. I served this one with penne pasta and the terrific Roasted Fennel and Tomato Sauce shown in the photo.

PHYLLO CHICKEN PROSCIUTTO MARGHERITA

1. Begin by butterfly cutting the chicken breasts and laying them flat on the cutting board. Alternatively you can place each chicken breast between 2 sheets of plastic wrap and pound the chicken out to a ½-inch thickness with a flat mallet. Season the chicken breasts with salt and pepper and rub the minced garlic over the surface of the chicken.

2. Lay the prosciutto on top of the chicken, almost covering it, then cover the prosciutto with fresh basil leaves. Place a 1½ oz rectangular piece of fresh mozzarella at one end of the chicken and roll the whole thing up.

3. The phyllo sheets I use measure about 12x18 inches, which I cut in half to make 12x9-inch sheets; I use 4 of these half-sheets per chicken breast. Brush each sheet with melted butter and stack 4 of them together.

4. Place one rolled chicken breast in the center of the shorter side of the phyllo sheets near the edge. Bring the two longer sides of the phyllo up over the ends of the chicken breasts and then roll the chicken breast up. (Similar to the method used to make spring rolls.) Place the wrapped chicken breast, seam side down, on a silicone or parchment-lined cookie sheet. Bake at 375°F for about 30-40 minutes, depending upon the size of the chicken breasts you use. I use a meat thermometer to test them and make sure the temperature at the center is 175°F or greater before taking them out of the oven. Let the chicken rest for 5-10 minutes before serving with the roasted fennel and tomato sauce and your favourite pasta.

ROASTED FENNEL AND TOMATO SAUCE

1. Preheat the oven to 350°F. Toss all ingredients together in a shallow baking dish and bake for about 60-70 minutes, stirring occasionally or until the fennel pieces are very soft, most of the liquid has cooked off, and the sauce reaches a good chunky consistency.

Oven Baked Panko Chicken Parmesan *with* Roasted Tomato Jam

SERVES 4

OVEN BAKED PANKO CHICKEN PARMESAN

4 large boneless **chicken breasts**

salt and **pepper** to season

flour for dredging

1 **egg** + 1 tbsp **water**, whisked to make an egg wash

panko crumbs

olive oil

angel hair pasta

grated **Parmesan cheese**

ROASTED TOMATO JAM

6 medium **vine ripened tomatoes**, diced

2 **cloves garlic**, minced

4 tbsp **extra virgin olive oil**

½ tsp **kosher salt**

½ tsp **freshly ground black pepper**

1 tsp **brown sugar**

The roasted tomato jam in this recipe is one I often make for bruschetta. I sometimes make large batches of this jam, just to have a couple of bottles on hand to use in other favourite recipes. This lower fat, baked version of chicken Parmesan is one of my favourite uses for the jam as it makes for a quick workday meal that's pretty healthy too, especially if you opt for a whole grain pasta.

OVEN BAKED PANKO CHICKEN PARMESAN

1. Preheat oven to 375°F. Season the chicken breasts with salt and pepper, dredge in flour, dip in the egg wash, and then roll in the panko crumbs. Place in a lightly oiled baking dish and lightly spray olive oil over the tops of the chicken breasts. Bake in the preheated oven for 45-50 minutes or until the chicken is completely cooked. Turn the chicken breasts once during the cooking time.

2. Slice the cooked chicken breasts and serve on angel hair pasta, topped with Roasted Tomato Jam (or your favourite tomato sauce) and grated Parmesan cheese. You can melt mozzarella over the top along with the Parmesan if you wish.

ROASTED TOMATO JAM

1. Preheat oven to 350°F. Toss the ingredients together in a shallow baking dish and bake for about an hour, stirring occasionally until most of the liquid has reduced and the tomatoes are the consistency of jam.

Baked Italian Chicken Cordon Bleu

SERVES 4

4 large chicken breasts, butterfly cut or pounded to about a ½-inch thickness

salt and pepper to season

2 cloves garlic, finely minced

6 oz provolone cheese

6 oz thinly sliced capicola ham

1½ cups bread, cracker, or cornflake crumbs

2 tbsp dried mixed Italian herbs

2 eggs + 2 tbsp water, whisked to make an egg wash

This is the kind of dish I like to serve at dinner parties simply because it can be prepared well in advance and then popped into the oven before your guests arrive. These were large breasts and still only took about an hour to cook completely. I use a meat thermometer to test the center. While poultry is generally well cooked at 185°F, I almost always cook these to 170° to 175° because the center is not chicken but cheese, and at 175°F, the provolone is melted perfectly while the chicken is not dried out. I also like to serve this particular stuffed chicken breast with Roasted Tomato Jam. That recipe is included with the Oven Baked Panko Chicken Parmesan recipe on page 28.

> **tip** > To lower the fat content even more, substitute extra-lean ham and low-fat cheese for the filling; still an outstanding meal.

1.   Butterfly cut and lay each chicken breast flat. Season with salt and pepper on both sides and rub ½ clove of minced garlic on the inside surface of the meat. Cut the provolone cheese into 4 sticks and wrap each one in 1½ oz capicola ham. Place the ham and cheese in the center of the flattened chicken and fold all sides of the breast meat toward the center to overlap. Flip the breast over so the overlapped edges are on the bottom.

2.   Preheat the oven to 350°F. Mix the crumbs with the Italian herbs. Dip the stuffed chicken breast into the egg wash and then into the seasoned crumbs. Place fold side down on a parchment-lined baking sheet and bake for about an hour or until the internal temperature of the breasts reaches 175°F on a meat thermometer.

HOMEMADE PASTA

4 cups durum semolina

2 cup all-purpose flour

8 large eggs, room temperature

THE SAUCE

3 tbsp olive oil

4 cloves garlic, minced

1½ lbs ground chicken (or pork or beef if you prefer)

½ lb chorizo sausage

1 small red onion, finely diced

2 large cans (32 oz can) crushed roma tomatoes

½ bunch fresh basil

1 tbsp ground or crushed fennel seed

1 tbsp oregano

1 whole bay leaf

1 large carrot, finely grated

½ cup finely diced celery

2 tbsp brown sugar

salt and pepper to taste

½ tsp chili flakes (optional)

RICOTTA FILLING

16 oz tub ricotta cheese

1 beaten egg

¼ tsp salt

¼ tsp pepper

¼ tsp freshly grated nutmeg

½ cup freshly grated Parmesan cheese

1 lb grated part-skim mozzarella cheese

Chicken Chorizo Lasagna

This recipe comes courtesy of Spouse, who is an excellent cook in her own right, meaning kitchen collaborations are a rule rather than an exception at our house. It was her idea to add chorizo to a lasagna, and this recipe is the result. I love chorizo sausage, and it adds great flavour to this delicious comfort-food pasta dish. You can use either fresh chorizo or finely chopped cured chorizo. Other spicy sausage can also be substituted too. Sometimes we even use leftover diced grilled chicken instead of ground chicken, which I actually prefer.

You can use store-bought lasagna noodles (fresh if possible) or make your own from the recipe provided below. If using dry lasagna noodles, par boil them for 5 minutes before assembling the dish unless, of course, they are the oven-ready variety.

HOMEMADE PASTA

1. Combine flour and durum semolina and make a well in the center. Crack your eggs into the well, and using a fork to beat the eggs, slowly begin to incorporate the flour into the eggs until everything is combined into a very stiff dough. You may add a little water to incorporate the dry ingredients if necessary, but be careful not to make your dough too loose; it should still be quite dense. Add a little extra flour if the dough is too sticky. The dough should be slightly stiffer than play dough.

2. Knead for 5-10 minutes on a bread board, cover in plastic wrap, and allow to rest for 20 minutes. Then knead a second time and allow to rest again. You can use a pasta machine to roll the dough into sheets about ⅛-inch thickness or just a regular rolling pin on a well-floured surface.

3. Boil pasta sheets for 1-2 minutes in salted water before using in the lasagna assembly. Lay the cooked pasta on a parchment paper-lined baking sheet while you assemble the lasagna.

> **tip** > Although I most often use ground chicken to make a meat sauce for this recipe, I have also had great success using leftover, lightly grilled and diced chicken instead. I just add the diced grilled chicken when assembling the layers of the lasagna.

THE SAUCE

1. In a large saucepan, sauté the minced garlic in 3 tbsp of olive oil for 1 minute. Add the ground chicken, chorizo sausage, and red onion. Cook until the meat has slightly browned.

2. Add the crushed roma tomatoes, fresh basil, crushed fennel seed, oregano, bay leaf, grated carrot, diced celery, brown sugar, salt and pepper (to taste), and chili flakes.

3. Slowly simmer for about 30-40 minutes or until the sauce thickens, stirring occasionally. Remove bay leaf.

RICOTTA FILLING

1. Preheat oven to 350°F. Mix together well the ricotta cheese, egg, salt, pepper, nutmeg, and Parmesan cheese.

2. Start constructing the lasagna by adding a cup of sauce to the bottom of a large lasagna pan. Add a layer of pasta, half the remaining sauce, another layer of pasta, then the ricotta filling, another layer of pasta, and the remaining sauce. Top with a final layer of pasta and the part-skim mozzarella cheese.

3. Bake in the preheated oven for about 1 hour, depending on the size of your lasagna pan. Let stand for 15-20 minutes before cutting and serving.

Creamy Parmesan Chicken Baked Rotini

SERVES 6

2½ cups whole milk

1½ cups chicken stock

⅓ cup butter

3 tbsp flour

¼ tsp black pepper

½ tsp sea salt

2 tbsp dry summer savoury (you can substitute 1 tsp dry thyme or 1 tsp dry sage)

2 tbsp Dijon mustard

3 cups uncooked rotini pasta

3 cups leftover cooked chicken (or turkey), cut in chunks

1 cup freshly grated Parmesan cheese

8 slices precooked bacon, cut in small pieces

3 cups grated low-fat mozzarella cheese

1 cup chopped button mushrooms (optional)

1 large roasted red bell pepper, chopped (optional)

This is one of our family's most loved comfort-food meals. It's a delicious way to stretch leftover roast chicken or even leftover supermarket rotisserie chicken into a fantastic, satisfying second supper. It's also a real leftover rescue recipe after a roast turkey dinner; turkey is equally or perhaps even more delicious than chicken in this recipe and a welcome winter warm-up meal after the holidays.

1. In a microwave, scald the whole milk and chicken stock to almost boiling.

2. In a medium saucepan over medium heat, cook the butter, flour, black pepper, and sea salt together for 2 minutes.

3. Whisking constantly, slowly pour in scalded milk and chicken stock. Continue to cook for 2 more minutes, stirring constantly. Then stir in the savoury and Dijon mustard.

4. In salted boiling water, cook, just to al dente, the rotini pasta. Drain and set aside.

5. Preheat oven to 350°F. Grease the bottom and sides of a large casserole dish. Place half of the cooked rotini pasta in the bottom of the dish. Layer the casserole with half the chicken, half the Parmesan cheese, half the bacon, and half the sauce. Repeat these layers and top with the grated mozzarella cheese. Bake in the preheated oven for about 45-60 minutes or until the casserole is bubbling and the top is golden brown.

Spice Rack Sage Butter Roast Chicken

SERVES 4–6

one 3 lb fresh chicken

⅓ cup butter

½ tsp freshly ground
black pepper

½ tsp kosher salt

1 tsp dried sage

½ tsp garlic powder

1 tsp onion powder

salt and pepper to season

1 small onion or large shallot,
cut in chunks

tip > Always let your roast chicken rest under a loose tent of aluminum foil for 10-15 minutes before carving. This step is essential for a juicy chicken; carving a chicken too early can result in drier meat, especially breast meat.

When it seems every celebrity chef out there is rediscovering the joys of a simple, perfectly roasted chicken, it never left my dinner table. A whole chicken is usually the most affordable way to serve fresh chicken, and although I do love using fresh herbs whenever I can, they do become pricy and sometimes unavailable during the winter months. This sage butter-based recipe demonstrates that pulling a few items from a well-stocked spice rack makes for a deliciously juicy, tender roast-chicken dinner as good as any other and likely much more economical too.

1. Preheat oven to 350°F. Beat together the butter, salt, pepper, sage, garlic powder, and onion powder until well combined.

2. Loosen the skin on the breasts and thighs of the chicken by very gently pushing your fingers between the skin and the meat. Be careful not to tear the skin.

3. Using about a tablespoon of the sage butter at a time, gently push it under the skin all over the chicken. Pat the outside of the chicken to distribute the butter as evenly as you can all over the bird.

4. Season the cavity of the chicken with salt and pepper and stuff the onion or shallot chunks inside.

5. Tie the chicken legs together with butcher string and tuck the wing tips under the chicken. Place the chicken on a roasting rack and roast *uncovered* until the chicken is completely cooked. It is not necessary to baste this chicken.

6. Chicken generally takes about 20 minutes per pound to be completely cooked, but sometimes an unstuffed bird will roast more quickly. I *always* use a meat thermometer to ensure the internal temperature at the center of the thickest part of the breast and thighs has reached at least 170° to 180°F. Avoid hitting a bone with your thermometer as this can give an inaccurate reading.

7. Let your chicken rest under a loose tent of aluminum foil for 10-15 minutes before carving.

While new chicken recipes are always popular on *Rock Recipes*, beef and pork dishes don't take a back seat among my most read posts. I always think of beef as a comfort-food staple, and although I've cut back on red meat in the past few years, nothing really says home cooking like a slow-cooked pot roast or the delicious stewed steak included here. Summer grilling season just wouldn't be the same without amazing burgers or that perfectly seared juicy steak. You may eat beef much less often than other meats, but when you do, why not make it something really delicious.

Pork, I think, has to be one of the most versatile ingredients in my cooking. I have a particular fondness for great pork-chop recipes and love a good center-loin pork roast as well. Pork tenderloin, as a quick and easy meal, is often overlooked as an option whether it is sliced into stir fried recipes or pan seared and quickly roasted. These pork recipes, plus a couple in the Quick and Easy Meals section, show that it can be as adaptable as chicken if given the opportunity.

Main Dishes: Beef *and* Pork

Stewed Steak

SERVES 4–6

3 lbs of sirloin, cross-rib, or blade steak (or similar cut)

salt and pepper to season

1 cup flour

2 tsp ground thyme

2 tsp fresh ground nutmeg

4-5 tbsp canola oil

5-6 cups of good beef stock (low-sodium stock if you are using store bought). You can substitute 1 cup of broth with a cup of red wine for an even richer gravy.

3 cloves garlic, minced

4 tbsp Worcestershire sauce

1 tsp ground black pepper

Here is one of our family's favourite winter comfort-food recipes that's pretty well fuss free and foolproof. It's an economical meal as well, making use of less expensive cuts of beef that benefit from slow braising. It takes just a few minutes to prepare the steak and then it's simply slowly braised in beef stock for a couple of hours until the meat is fall-apart tender and a rich gravy has formed. This excellent relaxing weekend meal satisfies practically everyone.

1. Season the steaks with salt and pepper. Mix together the flour, thyme, and nutmeg. Dredge the steaks in the flour mixture. Over medium heat, add enough canola oil to cover the bottom of your skillet. When the pan is heated, add the steaks and brown them on both sides. There's no need to cook them fully, just brown the surfaces well. Drain the excess oil from the skillet and deglaze the pan with a little beef stock before adding it to the steak in the roasting pan.

2. Preheat the oven to 300°F. Place the browned steaks in a covered roasting pan and add the beef stock, garlic, Worcestershire sauce, and black pepper.

3. Cover and slow cook the steaks in the preheated oven for 2-3 hours or until the meat is very tender and begins to fall apart. The flour used to brown the steaks helps thicken the gravy as it cooks. I like to skim any surface fat off the gravy before serving.

Chipotle Chili Sloppy Joes

SERVES 6–8

3 tbsp olive oil

3 cloves garlic, minced

1 medium red onion, finely diced

2½-3 lbs extra-lean ground beef

1½ cups tomato sauce

1½-2 cups canned kidney beans, rinsed

4 cups crushed tomatoes

2 roasted red bell peppers, chopped fine

3 ears of grilled corn, removed from cob

½ jalapeño pepper, minced (optional)

1 heaping tbsp cumin

2 heaping tbsp chili powder

1-3 tsp ground chipotle powder (depending on how spicy you like it)

2 tsp smoked paprika

3 tbsp molasses

salt and pepper to taste

Here's my favourite smoky flavoured chili recipe that makes the most amazing Sloppy Joes on homemade rolls. This chili is also very good on its own as a satisfying dinner. You can also serve it with tortilla chips as a dip when entertaining. Just add grated cheddar cheese on top and sour cream on the side.

1.   In a large pot, heat the olive oil and then add the garlic and red onion. Cook until the onions begin to soften then add ground beef and cook until brown, breaking the meat into small pieces. Add tomato sauce, kidney beans, crushed tomatoes, red peppers, grilled corn, jalapeño pepper, cumin, chili powder, chipotle powder, smoked paprika, molasses. Salt and pepper to taste.

2.   Simmer very gently over low heat for 1½-2 hours, stirring occasionally. Serve on toasted sour dough bread or rolls or, if serving alone, with tortilla chips and garnishes of grated cheddar cheese, sour cream, and guacamole.

Smoked Paprika and Balsamic Steak
with Garlic Herb Butter

SERVES 6–8

4 strip loin steaks

SMOKED PAPRIKA MARINADE

6 tbsp Worcestershire sauce

1½ tsp balsamic vinegar

1 tsp coarsely ground
black pepper

1½ tbsp olive oil

1 clove garlic, finely minced

3 tbsp smoked paprika

1 tsp honey

GARLIC HERB BUTTER

2–3 cloves garlic, minced

4 tbsp butter

1 cup soft butter

3–4 tbsp chopped fresh herbs
of your choice. I use chives,
oregano, and rosemary.

I've borrowed the steakhouse idea of melting a delicious herb and garlic butter over this succulent, perfectly seasoned grilled steak. The red colour from the paprika and the contrast of the beautiful creamy yellow butter makes for a beautiful presentation that will have any carnivore salivating.

I add a little honey to this marinade because the natural sugar caramelizes on the grill to create great grill marks and extra char flavour, but this is an optional ingredient.

> tip > As with all marinated steaks, marinating should take place in the fridge, but the steaks should be taken out of the fridge for 30-60 minutes before grilling. Grilling a cold steak can make it very difficult to cook the way you like it and can also make your steak tougher.

SMOKED PAPRIKA MARINADE

1. Mix together Worcestershire sauce, balsamic vinegar, pepper, olive oil, garlic, smoked paprika, and honey. Place the steaks and marinade in a Ziploc bag, push out as much air as possible, and seal. Work the marinade all over the steaks inside the bag. Marinate in the fridge for 1-3 hours, flipping the bag over at least once. Let the steaks come up to room temperature before grilling. Serve with melting garlic herb butter.

GARLIC HERB BUTTER

1. Begin by lightly sautéing together, over medium-low heat, the garlic and 4 tbsp butter. You only want to soften the garlic here and not brown it, so this will only take a minute or two. Don't have your pan too hot. Cool the garlic and then mix it together with the cup of soft butter and fresh herbs.

2. Place the prepared butter onto some plastic wrap and form into a log. Refrigerate until the shape of the log stays intact, but take the butter out of the fridge to warm up to room temperature before serving.

Roasted Garlic and White Cheddar Burgers *with* Beer and Bacon Jam

1 SERVING

ROASTED GARLIC AND WHITE CHEDDAR BURGER

2 cloves garlic, roasted and mashed

6 oz lean ground beef

1½ oz aged white cheddar, cut in 1cm cubes

pinch of kosher salt

⅛ tsp black pepper

½ tsp smoked paprika

¼ tsp ground dry thyme

1 tbsp Worcestershire sauce

BEER AND BACON JAM (MAKES ABOUT 2 CUPS)

½ lb smoked bacon

3 tbsp butter

6 large red onions, finely diced

6 cloves garlic, minced

1 tsp freshly ground black pepper

½ cup maple syrup

¼ cup balsamic vinegar

8 oz dark stout beer (or one cup brewed coffee works very well)

½ tsp dry thyme

While some recipes add grated cheese, I prefer to add small cubes of cheese into the ground-beef mixture, so it melts in little pockets and oozes out when you bite into the juicy burger.

The crowning glory of this burger is again one of my favourite grilling condiments—Beer and Bacon Jam! Sweet, smoky, slightly salty, and quite earthy, this delicious concoction is an amazing addition to grilled chops, steaks, chicken, and of course, burgers.

ROASTED GARLIC AND WHITE CHEDDAR BURGER

1.   Roasting garlic for this recipe is easy. Preheat oven to 375°F. Slice about a ¼ inch off the top of a head of garlic, place it on a square of aluminum foil, drizzle with a little olive oil, add a pinch of salt and pepper, and bring all the edges of the aluminum foil over the garlic head and squeeze it together to seal completely. Roast for about 35 minutes or until the garlic is completely softened, starting to turn golden brown, and the cloves are easily removed from the skins.

2.   For each burger, combine ground beef, white cheddar, kosher salt, pepper, roasted garlic, paprika, thyme, and Worcestershire sauce. Form into patties and cook on a hot grill or in a hot, lightly oiled cast iron pan until well done (internal temperature should read 160°F or higher). Serve on toasted crusty rolls topped with Beer and Bacon Jam.

BEER AND BACON JAM

1.   Cut the bacon into ¼-inch pieces and fry slowly over medium-low to medium heat until all the fat has been rendered out and the bacon is crispy, resembling bacon bits. Drain off all the fat and add butter, diced red onions, garlic, and ground black

pepper. Cook over medium-low heat for about 20 minutes until the onions have reduced considerably and caramelized. Then add the maple syrup, balsamic vinegar, beer (or coffee), and thyme. Simmer and reduce this mixture for several minutes until it reaches a jam-like consistency. Serve warm.

2. This jam will last for several days in a sealed container in the fridge or for much longer if you choose to make a large batch and follow proper canning/bottling procedures.

Maple Chipotle Barbeque Braised Ribs

MAPLE CHIPOTLE BARBEQUE SAUCE (MAKES ABOUT 3 CUPS)

3 tbsp olive oil

3 cloves garlic, chopped

1 medium red onion, chopped

2 cups plain tomato sauce

½ cup maple syrup

¼ cup apple cider vinegar

1-2 tsp ground chipotle powder (according to taste)

1 tsp black pepper

1 tbsp dry thyme

1½ tsp kosher salt

MAPLE CHIPOTLE BARBEQUE BRAISED RIBS

4-5 lbs pork ribs

1 tsp powdered ginger

2 tsp cumin

1 tbsp freshly ground black pepper

1 tbsp dry thyme

2 tbsp garlic powder

2 tbsp dry oregano

1½ tsp kosher salt

1 tsp ground chipotle powder

2 cups Maple Chipotle Barbeque Sauce

1 cup water

1 tsp chipotle powder

½ cup maple syrup

2 cloves garlic, minced

pinch of salt

This recipe really gives you a lot of ideas to work with. The outstanding recipe for homemade Maple Chipotle Barbeque Sauce can be used throughout the summer grilling season and beyond on steaks, chicken, chops, or burgers. As the grilling season wanes in your neck of the woods, use the sauce as a base to slowly braise pork ribs in the oven whenever a flavour reminder of summer barbeques will be welcome.

MAPLE CHIPOTLE BARBEQUE SAUCE

1. In a small saucepan, combine olive oil, chopped garlic, and red onion. Cook slowly over medium-low heat until well softened and beginning to caramelize. Then add tomato sauce, maple syrup, apple cider vinegar, chipotle powder, pepper, thyme, and salt.

2. Simmer slowly for about 20-30 minutes or until reduced by about ¼ the initial volume, stirring often. When cool, puree in a blender or food processor until smooth.

MAPLE CHIPOTLE BARBEQUE BRAISED RIBS

1. Combine ginger, cumin, pepper, thyme, garlic powder, oregano, kosher salt, and chipotle powder. Rub all over the surface of the ribs. (You can do this step the day before and let the ribs marinate in the spices overnight if you like to really infuse the flavour into the meat.) Place ribs in a single layer in a large covered roasting pan or on a cookie sheet that you will cover completely with aluminum foil. Cook for about 90 minutes at 300°F.

2. At this stage, cut the meat into individual ribs and place in a covered roasting pan. To the pan add the Maple Chipotle Barbeque Sauce, water, chipotle powder, maple syrup, garlic, and salt. Cover and return to the oven for 1½-2 hours or until they are very tender with the meat falling off the bones.

Steak *with* Smoked Mustard Chanterelle Sauce

SERVES 2

2 strip loin steaks

salt and pepper to season

2 cloves garlic, minced

6 tbsp butter

½ cup vegetable stock

4 tbsp smoked mustard

¾ cup chanterelle mushrooms

I've heard from many readers over the years who share my love of "steak night." We red-meat eaters have practically been forced underground in recent years, but I must stand and be counted. I love beef, and I'm not giving it up. I'm not eating it 3 times a week either. I do have some restraint.

This steak was inspired by two gifts I received from a couple in the neighbourhood. Angela gave me an interesting bottle of smoked mustard from a local specialty store, and her mushroom foraging husband, Mark, provided the beautiful little wild chanterelle mushrooms. It didn't take long for me to decide they could both be great together in a luscious sauce for steak.

1. Season the strip-loin steaks well with salt and pepper. Grill or pan sear the steaks to medium rare (or your preferred doneness) and let them rest for a few minutes while you prepare the sauce.

2. Sauté the garlic in 2 tbsp of butter over medium heat for only 1 minute or less to soften the garlic (don't let it brown). Add vegetable stock and smoked mustard. Simmer to reduce the sauce by about half.

3. Add the mushrooms for only about 1 minute, to heat them through. Remove the pan from the heat and add 4 tbsp of butter, one tbsp at a time, constantly stirring to slowly melt the butter. As soon as the butter is melted, serve immediately over the seared sliced steak.

Rum and Spice Glazed Pork Tenderloin

SERVES 4-6

2 to 3 lbs pork tenderloin

RUM GLAZE

2 tbsp olive oil

3 cloves garlic, minced

1 cup brown sugar

½ tsp + pinch of salt

½ tsp fresh minced ginger

4 oz dark rum

2-3 tbsp tabasco sauce

1 tsp minced jalapeno pepper (optional if you like a little extra heat)

SPICE RUB

1 tsp ground cinnamon

1 tsp ground ginger

2 tsp kosher salt

2 tsp ground cumin

½ tsp ground black pepper

2 tsp chili powder

The inspiration here came from a favourite dry-rubbed pork recipe. I made some additions to the original idea to bump up the spice and add a little more heat but, most importantly, added some dark rum to create a fantastic glaze. The pork tenderloin cooks quickly, making it an ideal quick workday dinner. Spouse declared it the best pork dish she'd ever eaten, so I have no hesitation using this as a dinner-party entree as well.

RUM GLAZE

1. In a small saucepan, over medium-low heat, add the olive oil and minced garlic. Sauté for only a minute until the garlic softens, and then add brown sugar, salt, ginger, rum, tabasco, and minced jalapeno. Simmer slowly for about 5 minutes until the glaze thickens slightly.

SPICE RUB

1. Preheat oven to 375°F. Mix together cinnamon, ginger, kosher salt, cumin, pepper, and chili powder, and rub over the entire surface of the pork tenderloins. To a skillet or frying pan on medium heat, add the vegetable oil, and then lightly brown the pork tenderloins on all sides.

2. Brush some of the glaze onto the pork tenderloin before placing it in the preheated oven for about 20-25 minutes, depending on the thickness of the tenderloins being used. I use a meat thermometer to test the meat and take the meat out of the oven when the internal temperature reaches 145° to 155°F. You can brush more glaze onto the meat halfway through the cooking time.

3. It's important to cover the meat with aluminum foil and let it rest for 10 minutes before slicing and serving. Spoon extra glaze over the pork when serving.

Brined Pan-Seared Pork Chops
with Maple Five-Spice Apples

SERVES 4

BRINED PAN-SEARED PORK CHOPS

6 cups of water

2 cups apple juice

½ cup brown sugar

¼ cup sea salt

2 tbsp black peppercorns

2 sprigs fresh thyme

3 cloves garlic, chopped

4 thick-cut pork chops (thin cuts will get over brined)

3 tbsp canola oil

MAPLE FIVE-SPICE APPLES

3 large Granny Smith apples— peeled, cored, and sliced thick

3 tbsp butter

½ tsp dry thyme

4 tbsp raisins

⅓ cup apple juice

¼ cup maple syrup

1 tsp five-spice powder

juice of ½ a lemon

3 tbsp apple cider vinegar

This recipe just says, "Great cold weather comfort food!" The brining of the pork chops is optional, of course, and should not be done for longer than a couple of hours, but the process imparts a fantastic deep-seasoned flavour and makes the chops extra plump and juicy.

The fragrantly spiced apples achieve a tart balance between the maple syrup, apple cider vinegar, and lemon juice, making them the perfect accompaniment to the pan-seared pork chops.

BRINED PAN-SEARED PORK CHOPS

1.   For the brining liquid, stir together water, apple juice, brown sugar, sea salt, black peppercorns, thyme, and chopped garlic until the salt and sugar dissolves. Soak the 4 large, thick-cut pork chops in the brine for no longer than 2 hours. Remove from the brine and pat dry.

2.   Preheat oven to 400°F. Heat a cast-iron pan or heavy bottom, oven-safe frying pan over medium-high heat, and add the 3 tbsp canola oil. Pan sear the chops for about 2 minutes per side. Place pan in hot oven for 10 minutes to finish cooking. Cooking time may be longer depending on the thickness of your chops. Use a meat thermometer to get the internal temperature to at least 145°F.

MAPLE FIVE-SPICE APPLES

1.   Sauté the apples in butter over medium heat to get them warmed. Then add thyme, raisins, apple juice, maple syrup, five-spice powder, lemon juice, and apple cider vinegar. Simmer until the sauce reduces to a glaze-like consistency. Serve warm over the cooked pork chops.

PORK CHIMICHANGAS

2 roma tomatoes, de-seeded and diced small

1 tbsp olive oil

½ tsp chipotle powder (or 1 tsp chili powder)

¼ tsp cumin

¼ tsp black pepper

pinch of salt

3 cups cooked pork, very thinly sliced and roughly chopped

8 oz Monterey Jack cheese, cut in four 6-inch strips

4 flour tortillas, 10-12 inches in diameter

AVOCADO PINEAPPLE SALSA

1½ cups fresh golden pineapple, diced small

1 clove garlic, minced

1 tbsp lemon juice

½ red onion, diced

1 tbsp finely chopped jalapeño pepper

1 tsp salt

½ tsp coarse ground black pepper

1 tsp ground cumin

1 tbsp brown sugar

¼ cup chopped fresh cilantro or basil

½ red bell pepper, diced small

1 large avocado, diced

Pork Chimichangas *with* Avocado Pineapple Salsa

This treat is actually another leftover rescue recipe made from roasted center loin of pork. The recipe can be made from leftover grilled pork chops or pork tenderloin as well. If you're not a pork eater, chicken is an easy substitution and just as delicious.

The leftover pork stays moist and juicy inside the chimichangas, helped along by some fresh diced tomatoes and just the right amount of spice. The avocado and pineapple salsa provides a fresh, delicious counterpoint to the crispy tortilla shell, melting cheese, and tasty pork. Now that's leftovers without complaints!

PORK CHIMICHANGAS

1. Toss together the tomatoes, olive oil, chipotle powder, cumin, salt, and pepper. Add the chopped pork and toss together well.

2. Place the cheese strips in the center of the tortillas. Add ¼ of the pork mixture beside the cheese. Bring two opposite sides of the tortilla toward the center (they don't need to meet). Begin rolling from one of the ends, making sure the seam is on the bottom of the chimichanga.

3. Heat oil to 325°F in a deep fryer and place the chimichangas seam side down in the basket. Lower into the hot oil and fry until golden brown. Serve with the Avocado Pineapple Salsa.

AVOCADO PINEAPPLE SALSA

1. Add all ingredients together and toss well in a glass bowl. Let stand for about 2 hours before serving, stirring occasionally. Serve at room temperature.

Apple Sausage Stuffed Pork Loin

SERVES 6-8

APPLE SAUSAGE

2 medium apples, coarsely grated

1 lb coarsely ground pork shoulder

2 oz finely chopped or ground smoked bacon (uncooked)

1 tsp brown sugar

1 tsp salt

½ tsp coarsely ground black pepper

¼ tsp chilli flakes

¼ tsp ground nutmeg

1 tsp onion powder

½ tsp garlic powder

1 tsp ground sage

½ tsp ground thyme

STUFFED PORK LOIN

3-4 lbs center-loin pork roast

salt and pepper to season

2 tbsp olive oil

Homemade sausage doesn't have to be complicated and doesn't necessarily have to be stuffed into casings. The Easy Homemade Breakfast Sausage patties recipe in the brunch chapter if this book (see page 188) is an excellent example. Here, an easy to make apple sausage creates an excellent stuffing for a Sunday pork-roast dinner. Apples and pork always go well together, which makes this sausage a natural choice.

> tip > I often make the apple sausage a day in advance so the seasoning has plenty of time to penetrate the ground pork, resulting in improved flavour.

APPLE SAUSAGE

1.   Squeeze the grated apples in your hands to remove as much of the juice as you can. Toss together with the pork and bacon and divide into 3 portions.

2.   For the sausage seasoning mix, combine the brown sugar, salt, pepper, chilli flakes, nutmeg, onion powder, garlic powder, sage, and thyme.

3.   Place the first ⅓ of the meat and apple mixture in a large bowl. Sprinkle evenly with ⅓ of the seasoning mix, add the next ⅓ of the meat mixture, the next ⅓ of the seasoning, then finally the last of the meat and seasoning mixes. Using this method, before mixing the meat and seasoning together, ensures an even dispersal of spices throughout the sausage.

4.   Using your hands, mix the sausage together well, cover with plastic wrap, and store it in the fridge until ready to use.

STUFFED PORK LOIN

1. Preheat oven to 375°F. Place the roast fat side up on a cutting board and cut a slit in the side of the roast about ¾ of the way to the opposite side. I like this method of stuffing the side of a pork roast because the sausage is immediately exposed to the heat and begins to cook instantly, ensuring it becomes well cooked at the center without overcooking the pork. I still cook it to a center temperature of 175°F just to be sure, but I find this method cooks faster and more evenly.

2. Stuff the apple sausage into the opening. Tie the roast together with several pieces of butcher string. Rub the outside of the roast with the olive oil to make it brown more evenly. Season the roast with salt and pepper on all sides. Place on a roasting rack and open roast for about 1½ hours or until the internal temperature at the center reaches 175°F on a meat thermometer. This is a higher recommended internal temperature for roast pork, but is the recommended temperature for sausage. Let the roast rest for 15 minutes or so when it comes out of the oven before slicing and serving.

Coming from Newfoundland—and having always had family members working in the fishery—fish and seafood have consistently been big favourites in our family circle. Growing up, fish was always something very simply prepared. Cod was mostly poached, pan fried, or as my dad still does, stewed as a whole fish with onions and potatoes. When in season, crab boils were an exciting pastime too, with my dad forced to use a camp stove outside because Mom would claim she couldn't get the smell out of the house for days afterward. Table tops would be covered with newspapers as family and friends started cracking big meaty legs of Atlantic snow crab, leaving a heap of shells at the center of the table.

The most exotic seafood dish I ate as a child was an occasional cod au gratin, and although it upsets the sensibilities of those who balk at the suggestion of fish and cheese together, it's still one of the most searched for seafood dishes on *Rock Recipes*. Through the years, I've done a lot more experimenting with seafood dishes, and these recipes represent some of the best successes, which have turned out to be fan favourites too.

Main Dishes: Seafood

Cod au Gratin

SERVES 6

2 cups whole milk

3 tbsp butter

3 tbsp flour

2 tbsp Dijon mustard

1 tsp summer savoury
(dill or tarragon make good
substitutions)

1 tsp finely grated lemon zest

salt and pepper to taste

½ cup shredded Parmesan
cheese

3 lbs fresh cod fillets

1½ cups shredded mild cheddar
cheese

1 cup cracker crumbs

1 tbsp olive oil

Some people flinch at the suggestion of fish and cheese together, but this is one of the most requested recipes on *Rock Recipes* and a dish that's been made here in Newfoundland for a long time. I think the mild neutral flavour of cod actually lends itself well to being paired with cheese. As long as the cheese flavour is not too strong, you can substitute many mild cheeses like mozzarella or even gruyere to make your own favourite version of this recipe.

1.   Preheat the oven to 350°F. Scald the milk in the microwave for about 4-5 minutes until just under the boiling point. Meanwhile, in a medium saucepan, add the butter and flour and cook together for 2 minutes. Slowly pour in the scalded milk, whisking constantly. Cook until the sauce begins to thicken. Add the summer savoury, lemon zest, Dijon mustard, and season with salt and pepper to taste. Add the Parmesan cheese just before pouring on the fish.

2.   Arrange the fish in the bottom of a greased 9x9-inch baking dish or in individual gratin dishes. Pour the sauce over the fish. Top with the cheddar cheese.

3.   Mix the cracker crumbs with the olive oil (and an extra pinch of summer savoury if you like) and sprinkle over the cheese. Bake for 45-60 minutes in the preheated oven until bubbling and the top has evenly browned. Individual gratin dishes should take about 25-30 minutes, just check the center to see that the fish has fully cooked.

CAJUN SPICE MIX
3 tbsp smoked paprika

3 tbsp paprika

3 tbsp onion powder

2 tbsp garlic powder

1 tbsp chili powder

2 tbsp dried oregano

2 tbsp dried basil

1½ tbsp ground thyme

½ tbsp crushed chili flakes

1 tbsp cayenne pepper

1 tbsp coarsely ground black pepper

1 tbsp white pepper

1 tbsp celery salt

2 tbsp kosher salt

GRILLED CAJUN SHRIMP
2 or 3 dozen large shrimp

kosher salt to season

Cajun Spice Mix

SAUCE
½ cup low-fat strained yogurt (or ⅓ cup whipping cream)

3-4 cloves garlic, minced

3 tbsp olive oil

4 cups canned crushed tomatoes

2 anchovy fillets, chopped

salt and pepper to season

2 tbsp capers

1 tbsp brown sugar

2 tbsp balsamic vinegar

½ tsp chili flakes (more or less to taste)

1 tbsp Cajun Spice Mix

4 tbsp chopped fresh basil

Creamy Cajun Shrimp Puttanesca

This is my kind of meal: a delicious, spicy, satisfying plate of pasta with succulent grilled Cajun shrimp. It's based on a restaurant meal I tried a couple of years ago where chicken was used instead of the shrimp in this Cajun-Italian fusion dish, and you could very easily substitute boneless skinless chicken breast strips in this recipe if you prefer. The original recipe added Parmesan cheese, which you can also add if you prefer and especially if you are using chicken. The original sauce was also finished with cream. I've used some strained yogurt to keep the fat content low. If you're using yogurt, you will need to strain it for an hour or so beforehand as instructed below.

CAJUN SPICE MIX

1. Mix the ingredients together in preparation for the shrimp. Store any leftover rub in an airtight plastic container. Great for grilled steaks and chops too.

GRILLED CAJUN SHRIMP

1. Season the shrimp with the salt and then roll them in several tablespoons of the Cajun Spice Mix. Lightly grill the shrimp for only about a couple of minutes per side. Set aside to add to the sauce when it's ready.

SAUCE

1. Place a coffee filter in a colander or mesh strainer. Add the yogurt and allow to stand in the fridge over a bowl to drain for an hour or two.

2. Sauté the garlic in olive oil for only a minute before adding the anchovies and tomatoes. Season with salt and pepper. Add the capers, brown sugar, balsamic vinegar, about 1 tbsp of the Cajun Spice Mix, and cook until the sauce begins to thicken to a jam-like consistency. Add the basil in the last minute or so of cooking along with the grilled Cajun shrimp and strained yogurt (or whipping cream). Simmer for just 1-2 minutes before serving.

Salmon Sweet Potato Cakes

MAKES 8 LARGE SALMON CAKES OR ABOUT 24 HORS D'OEUVRE-SIZED MINI CAKES

4 large russet potatoes

3 large sweet potatoes

½ bulb roasted garlic

1½ lbs salmon

1 beaten egg

6 tbsp chopped fresh tarragon

salt and pepper to taste

1½ cups Panko crumbs

canola oil for frying

The idea for this recipe was swimming around in my head for a while, and when I finally got around to executing it, the result was quite delicious. The mixture of sweet potatoes and white potatoes allows the mixture to be formed into cakes, which is not so easy if you use only sweet potatoes.

These make a terrific lunch or appetizer dish, served with a simple green salad or in a smaller version as yummy party hors d'ouevres.

1. Preheat oven to 375°F. Wrap all the potatoes in aluminum foil and bake for about 1 hour until fork tender, and let them cool completely. You can roast the garlic at the same time using the same method, but take the garlic out of the oven after 30 minutes.

2. Poach the salmon in gently boiling salted water for about 10 minutes. Cool completely, remove bones and skin, and break into bite-sized pieces.

3. Remove the cooled sweet potatoes and russet potatoes from their skins and mash them together. Mash the roasted garlic cloves with a fork before adding them to the mashed sweet and russet potatoes. Add the beaten egg and stir well. Fold in the tarragon and salmon gently. You don't want to break up the salmon too much as you blend it into the mashed potatoes. Season with salt and pepper.

4. Chill the mashed potato and salmon mixture for an hour or so then form into balls about the size of a small orange. Roll the balls in Panko crumbs and pat them into 1-inch thick cakes and fry in canola oil over medium-low heat until golden brown. Serve with a squeeze of lemon or lime.

Pan-Seared Salmon
with Dijon Maple Butter Sauce

SERVES 4

SMOKED PAPRIKA MARINADE
four 6-8 oz salmon fillet pieces

2-3 tbsp canola oil

salt and pepper to season

DIJON MAPLE BUTTER SAUCE
2 cloves garlic, minced

4 + 1 tbsp butter

¾ cup white wine

2 tbsp Dijon mustard

2 tbsp maple syrup

3 tbsp capers

¼ tsp cracked black pepper

pinch of salt

A friend once asked me for a recipe for salmon to serve at a dinner party that was uncomplicated to prepare in very little time. No problem. Oh, and could it be really tasty too? Again, no problem. This simply seasoned and pan-seared salmon gets served with a luscious, easy to make butter sauce with just a few simple ingredients. This recipe is easily prepared in about 20 minutes, making it suitable for double duty as a worthy dinner-party dish or a quick and easy workday dinner.

tip > In practically any sauce that includes butter, reserving a tablespoon or so to stir in at the very end will almost always improve the taste and body of the sauce.

SMOKED PAPRIKA MARINADE

1. Salmon fillets about 1-inch thick or more work best for pan searing. Heat the oil in a skillet over medium-high heat. Get the pan fully heated before adding the canola oil. Season the salmon fillets with salt and pepper and add them to the hot pan. Pan sear for about 3-5 minutes per side, depending upon the thickness of the fillets. Only turn the fillets once. Pay attention to the time the salmon is seared on the first side. If you look at the side of the fillet as it cooks, you can easily see the colour change as the fish cooks. When the lighter colour of the cooked salmon reaches halfway through the thickness of the fillet, then it's time to turn them. Simply cook them for an equal amount of time on the second side or a little less if you prefer salmon to be slightly pinker at the center. Remove from pan and hold in a 200°F oven for just a few minutes while you prepare the sauce.

DIJON MAPLE BUTTER SAUCE

1. Drain the excess oil from the pan and return the pan to the stove. Add the minced garlic and 4 tbsp butter. Cook only until the garlic is just softened but not browned; only a minute or so will do. Then add the white wine, Dijon mustard, maple syrup, capers, pepper, and salt.

2. Simmer quickly to reduce the sauce until it starts to thicken. This should only take 3-4 minutes. Remove from heat and stir in 1 tbsp butter to finish the sauce.

3. Spoon the sauce over the fillets before serving.

Cod à la Empire

SERVES 6

2-3 lbs fresh cod fillets

SAVOURY ALMOND STUFFING
2 cloves garlic, minced

½ small red onion, diced small

3 tbsp olive oil

3 cups whole-wheat bread,
cut in ½-inch dice

2 tbsp chopped chives

½ tsp cracked black pepper

3 tbsp dried summer savoury
(tarragon, dill, or basil make good
substitutes)

¼ cup melted butter

1-2 oz warm water

½ cup chopped toasted almonds

8-10 oz of very thinly sliced
prosciutto

QUICK TOMATO COMPOTE
4 cloves garlic, minced

6 tbsp olive oil

8 large ripe tomatoes, diced

2 tbsp brown sugar

½ tsp crushed chili sauce or
chili flakes

salt and pepper to season

6 tbsp balsamic vinegar

This delectable recipe was developed to celebrate the fourth anniversary of my *Rock Recipes* blog and gets its name from the avenue I live on in St. John's. It features two of my favourite local ingredients—fresh North Atlantic cod and *the* favourite Newfoundland grown herb, summer savoury, which has been the essential element in poultry stuffing in every kitchen in the province for decades. Because all of the prep work can be done in advance and the fish popped into a hot oven at the last minute, it's an ideal dinner-party dish and one that gets served up repeatedly at my table.

> **tip** > Tail sections of cod are best because they're thinner, making them easier to roll up, and the triangular sections can be placed beside each other in opposite directions to form a rectangle. If the cod fillet is quite thick, simply slice it in half horizontally to create two thinner pieces.

1. Prepare six fish portions in roughly 5x7-inch rectangles. Overlap slightly if using two pieces of fish to prepare the portion.

SAVOURY ALMOND STUFFING

1. Preheat oven to 400°F. Sauté the garlic and onion in the olive oil until softened but not browned. Remove from heat and toss together with the cut whole-wheat bread, chives, pepper, summer savoury, ¼ cup melted butter, warm water, and toasted almonds.

2. Squeeze handfuls of the stuffing into sausage-shaped portions the width of the fish fillet and place at one end. Roll the fillet rectangle all the way around the stuffing. Lay out slices of the prosciutto again in about a 5x7-inch rectangle and place the prepared cod and stuffing at one end. Roll the prosciutto tightly around the cod and place in a lightly oiled shallow glass baking dish. Do not crowd the portions in the baking dish; allow at least an inch or two between the portions for good air circulation in the oven. If cooking all six portions at once, use two 9x13-inch or similar-size glass baking dishes. Crowding the portions in the pan will not allow the prosciutto to seal the portions properly and the cod will dry out.

3. Bake the portions for 25 minutes. Remove from oven and let rest for 10 minutes before serving with warm tomato compote.

QUICK TOMATO COMPOTE

1. Sauté the garlic in the oil over medium heat for just a minute before adding the tomatoes, brown sugar, chili sauce, salt, and pepper. Continue to cook until the tomatoes soften and the compote reduces to a jam-like consistency. Add the balsamic vinegar in the final minute or two of cooking before serving.

Five-Spice Salmon Teriyaki

four 6-oz **salmon fillet** portions,
about 1½ inches thick

MARINADE

½ cup **low-sodium soya sauce**

½ cup **honey**

½ cup **brown sugar**

¼ tsp **Chinese five-spice powder**
(or cinnamon)

2 tsp **sesame oil**

4 tbsp **rice wine vinegar**
(or apple cider vinegar)

1 oz piece **fresh ginger**,
very finely grated (freezing ginger
makes it easier to grate)

½ tsp freshly **ground black pepper**

2 cloves **garlic**, minced

2 tbsp **olive oil**

¼ cup **water**

suggestion >
• Very good served with jasmine rice.

We normally eat our fish quite simply prepared at our house. Baked, pan fried, or lightly poached with a squeeze of lemon is usually enough for me, but sometimes a change of pace is in order, and this great baked salmon teriyaki is one of the ways we really enjoy pumping up the flavour of that beautiful fish. Chinese five-spice powder gives this recipe a little extra exotic flavour, which goes extremely well with the teriyaki flavours and the delicate taste of the fresh salmon.

> tip > Whether you're pan frying or baking fish, crowding too may portions into a small space will almost always guarantee the finished product will be too dry. If necessary, use two pans to sear your fish portions or a larger baking sheet in the oven to ensure there's plenty of room for air circulation. When fish pieces touch, they create a steaming environment that can leach out much of the moisture in the flesh. Give it a little space and you'll notice the difference.

MARINADE

1. Mix together the soya sauce, honey, brown sugar, five-spice powder (or cinnamon), sesame oil, vinegar, grated ginger, and black pepper. Place the salmon fillets in a Ziploc bag with the marinade and let rest in the fridge for about an hour. Preheat oven to 425°F.

2. In a small saucepan, lightly sauté the minced garlic in the olive oil. Drain the marinade from the fish and add to the garlic and oil. Add ¼ cup water and simmer until the sauce thickens to a glaze-like consistency.

3. Place the marinated salmon fillets on a parchment-lined baking sheet and bake for about 15 minutes. At this point, begin brushing the marinade on the salmon and returning it to the oven for a couple of minutes between coatings. I normally glaze it about 3 times. You can always add more of the sauce to the fish when serving.

Soy and Ginger Grilled Scallops

SERVES 4

1½ lbs scallops

2 small bell peppers, any colour or mix them up

3 or 4 bamboo skewers

MARINADE

½ cup low-sodium soy sauce

¼ cup lemon juice

3 tbsp peanut oil

few drops toasted sesame oil

2 tbsp honey

2 tbsp finely grated fresh ginger root

½ tsp Chinese five-spice powder

1 clove garlic, finely minced

pinch of salt

pinch of black pepper

Scallops are my favourite seafood. Period. I've often had them at their very freshest and best, only hours after being plucked from the ocean floor. I love them prepared in practically any way, from tempura battered to practically raw in a lime ceviche. During the summer months I also love them simply marinated in any number of ways and then lightly grilled.

This recipe is particularly tasty and very simple to prepare. It makes a perfect appetizer course for a barbeque dinner party or served on a fresh summer salad for a light lunch or dinner meal. If you like, you can make double the marinade and with one half add some rice wine vinegar to make a terrific salad dressing too.

1. For the marinade, mix the ingredients together and marinate the scallops for no longer than 20 minutes; longer than this can allow the citric acid in the lemon juice to break down the surface of the scallops and dry them out when cooked. While the scallops are marinating you can also soak 3 or 4 bamboo skewers in water to prepare them for the grill.

2. Push the scallops onto the pre-soaked bamboo skewers. If you like, you can alternate the scallops with pieces of bell peppers and/or red onions.

3. Place the scallop skewers onto a preheated grill on medium heat and grill for only 2 to 3 minutes per side, depending on the size of scallops you're using.

Baked Cod *with* Beans and Chorizo

SERVES 4

1½ lbs cod fillets (or your favourite white fish)

2 cloves garlic, minced

1 tbsp olive oil

½ cup low-fat chorizo sausage (chicken or turkey chorizo is good)

2 cups cherry tomatoes, halved or quartered

2 tbsp fresh thyme

½ tsp salt

½ tsp black pepper

2½ cups canned 5 bean mix (or just use your favourite beans)

½ cup mixed pitted olives

½ cup white wine

This healthy meal is bursting with colour, flavour, and plenty of nutrition. It's also a quick and easy meal you should have little problem getting on the table in about a half-hour or so.

1. Preheat oven to 375°F. Soften the garlic in the oil over medium heat. Add the chorizo and stir fry for a minute before adding the rest of the ingredients and bringing to a simmer.

2. Add the cod fillets to a baking dish in a single layer. Season with salt and pepper. Add the simmered beans and sauce and place in the oven for only about 20-25 minutes or until the cod pieces are cooked through.

Pan-Seared Scallops *with* Fettuccine in Bacon Fennel Cream Sauce

SERVES 4

4 slices crisp cooked bacon

2 cloves garlic, finely chopped

12 oz whipping cream

2 tbsp very finely chopped fennel (you can substitute ½ tsp ground fennel seed)

salt and pepper to taste

4 tsp extra virgin olive oil

2 dozen large scallops

350 g package fresh fettuccine pasta, cooked

One of my friends calls this a "Boss is coming to dinner" recipe. It ticks a lot of boxes for a simple dish that makes an impact. It uses quality fresh ingredients, is quick to prepare, and has multiple layers of flavours from the smoky bacon to the delicate scallops and slightly anise flavour of the fennel. This delicious dish is sure to impress any dinner guest, especially if she signs your paycheck.

1.   Chop bacon into small pieces and cook until crisp in a large sauté pan. Drain and discard the fat. Return bacon to the same sauté pan and add garlic, whipping cream, fennel, and salt and pepper to taste. Stir well, scraping the bottom of the pan to deglaze the bacon from the pan. Simmer for a few minutes until the sauce slightly thickens.

2.   In a separate heavy bottomed sauté pan, heat olive oil until very hot on medium-high heat. Lightly salt the scallops and sear them in the olive oil for only about 2 minutes per side. Sear the scallops a few at a time and don't crowd the pan. Serve the scallops over the fettuccine and spoon the sauce over the top.

Super Crispy Fish and Chips

SERVES **4**

SUPER CRISPY FISH

1 cup all-purpose flour

1 cup rice flour + more for dredging

1 tsp salt

½ tsp freshly ground black pepper

1 large egg, lightly beaten

2¼ cups cold soda water or beer

canola oil or peanut oil for deep frying

2 lbs of boneless skinned cod fillets

salt and pepper to season

LIME AND CAPER TARTAR SAUCE

1 cup plain mayonnaise

2 tsp chopped capers

2 tsp sweet pickle relish

1 tsp honey

1 tsp Worcestershire sauce

1 tsp chopped lime zest

juice of ½ lime

pinch of black pepper

TWICE FRIED FRENCH FRIES

2 lbs potatoes

canola oil for deep frying

There's no better comfort food for a Newfoundlander than fish and chips. Everyone has their own opinions on where to get the best "fee and chee," but with a little effort you can make your own. I like this version very much. The trick to getting it right is the consistency of the batter. Most homemade versions I've tried use a batter that's too thick. Many recipes call for a batter that is similar in consistency to pancake batter. In my experience the batter needs to be thinner or the fried fish pieces will become soggy quite quickly. If your fish batter is not crispy enough when cooked, try thinning the batter with a little more liquid. Pre-heating the oil to the proper temperature is also very important or the fish will absorb too much of the oil while cooking.

Using part rice flour in the batter is also a sure fire way to ensure a crispy, light batter. I love a little homemade tarter sauce with my fee and chee and the lime and caper version in the included recipe is a particular favourite.

SUPER CRISPY FISH

1. Combine dry ingredients. Add the egg and soda water and whisk together just until the liquid is incorporated. Small lumps in the batter are not a problem.

2. Preheat the canola oil-filled deep fryer to 375°F. Cut the fish into about 8 pieces. Season the fish with salt and pepper on both sides. Dredge the fish pieces in rice flour to help the batter stick to the fillets. Dip the pieces into the batter and carefully drop them into the deep fryer. Fry for a few minutes, about 5 is fine, depending on the thickness of the fillets, just until golden brown on both sides. Drain on a wire rack placed over a cookie sheet. Serve immediately.

3. If you have to fry the fish in more than one batch at a time, hold the fish in a 200°F oven on the draining rack to provide air circulation all the way around the fried fish pieces to prevent the fish from getting soggy.

4. Serve with Twice Fried French Fries and Lime and Caper Tartar Sauce.

LIME AND CAPER TARTAR SAUCE

1. Stir all ingredients together until well blended. Let sit in the fridge for 1 hour or more to allow the flavours to meld before serving with the fried fish.

TWICE FRIED FRENCH FRIES

1. Twice frying French fries assures that you can quickly give them a second fry to crisp them as soon as all the fish is fried. This is quite helpful in terms of time management when preparing this meal, especially when serving a large number of people. The first fry also ensures the residual heat in the fries will fully cook them through without browning too quickly for perfect fries every time.

2. Wash or peel the potatoes well and cut into French fries. Cover with hot water while the canola oil heats in the deep fryer to 350°F. Dry the potatoes on a clean dishtowel and add them to the oil. Turn the heat down to 325° on the deep fryer. Fry just until the French fries get the first hint of golden colour then take them out immediately and drain on a wire rack over a cookie sheet.

3. Just before serving, make sure the oil is at 375°F, then add the fries back into the deep fryer for just a few minutes until they become crispy and golden brown. Sprinkle with a little salt as soon as they come out of the oil.

Shrimp and Bacon Pad Thai

8 oz package of rice noodles, soaked and drained

8 slices thick-cut smoked bacon

2 tbsp peanut oil or vegetable oil

3 cloves garlic, minced

½ shallot, minced

1 lb shrimp, shelled and deveined

salt and pepper to season

2 large eggs, slightly beaten

2 tsp toasted sesame oil

2 tbsp rice wine vinegar

2 tbsp honey

juice of 1 lime

2 tbsp Sriracha sauce (or to taste)

2 tsp light soy sauce

1½ tbsp fish sauce

3 green onions, cut in ½-inch pieces

2 tbsp tender lemon grass shoots, sliced very thin

½ small red bell pepper, cut in thin pieces

toasted peanuts or cashews

4 tbsp chopped cilantro or flat leaf parsley

8 lime wedges

Noodle dishes are pretty popular right now, but they've always been common at our house. On one trip to Boston last year, the family had a delicious lunch at Ming Tsai's Blue Dragon Restaurant. That's where I first had a version of this pad thai dish featuring scallops and bacon, which I thought was a little odd. I mean, I don't think *bacon* when I think of Asian cuisine, but the meal was quite delectable. Scallops and bacon are never a bad combination, and I like food that breaks the rules, so I decided to try my own version. I used shrimp instead because, although scallops are my favourite seafood, the family are more inclined toward shrimp. You could easily use small scallops instead if you prefer. This is a mildly hot pad thai. If I'm making this for myself, I add chillies with the other veggies at the end, and you can too if you prefer a hotter version.

> tip > With stir-fried dishes, it's important to prepare and measure all ingredients beforehand. These dishes come together very quickly, and you won't have time to measure out individual ingredients as you cook. I use small ramekins or dessert bowls to hold premeasured ingredients right beside the stove to quickly add them as needed.

1. Soak the rice noodles as directed on the package. I've used some wide noodles in my version, which take about 40 minutes to pre-soak. Smaller noodles will take much less time; just use the package as your guide. Don't soak them for longer than recommended. You don't want mushy noodles in your pad thai.

2. Cut the bacon in ½-inch pieces and gently fry until crisp. Drain off the fat and set aside.

3. Heat your wok over high heat and add peanut oil (or vegetable oil), garlic, minced shallot, shrimp, and salt and pepper to season. Stir fry the shrimp for 1-2 minutes then remove them to a plate and set aside. Remove as much of the garlic and shallot as you can as well.

4. Into the hot wok, add the eggs and a pinch of salt and pepper. Stir fry the egg to scramble it, chopping it in small pieces as you go.

5. Quickly add toasted sesame oil, rice wine vinegar, honey, lime juice, Sriracha sauce, soy sauce, and fish sauce. Simmer for 30 seconds or so before adding the shrimp, soaked rice noodles, and bacon to the wok along with the green onion, lemon grass, and red pepper.

6. Stir fry for a few additional minutes to heat all the ingredients well and make sure the noodles are soft and tender.

7. Serve with a garnish of toasted peanuts or cashews and a sprinkle of chopped cilantro or flat leaf parsley. Add lime wedges on top when serving to squeeze over the plate before eating.

In a time when family dinners are relegated to weekends for for many busy folks, if even then, our family still makes our sit-down dinner a priority at the end of every day. This doesn't happen by accident. Flexibility and planning are the secrets to this quality-time ritual.

We're fortunate enough to live fairly close to both our workplaces, but with a busy family life that includes evening dance or music lessons, among a myriad of other activities for the kids, we don't necessarily have a set dinner time. This is where planning and flexibility meet. We always plan for the next day's activities, and if dinner has to be an hour or so later than normal, so be it. Quick and easy workday meals are key, and whenever one evening's cooking can spill over into the next with leftovers, that's a bonus too.

I always say that if you're deciding what's for dinner at 5 o'clock, you are almost guaranteed to be eating out of a bucket. While a take-out pizza is not an unknown occurrence at our house, it is a bit of a rarity, and pre-packaged, processed meals are non-existent as we always try to eat good, real food together as a family. Many *Rock Recipes* readers have responded by stating that they're not happy with the way their own families eat, but that recipes like these, plus a little planning, help make moving away from fast food and processed meals easier than they ever thought.

Quick *and* Easy Dinners

Lemon Chicken Asparagus Spaghetti

SERVES 4

4 grilled chicken breasts, fully cooked

½ lb dry spaghetti

3 cloves garlic, minced

3 tbsp olive oil

¼ cup butter

juice and finely grated zest of 1 lemon

2 tbsp chopped fresh oregano

½ cup white wine (or chicken stock)

1 tbsp Dijon mustard

2 cups chopped fresh asparagus

1 small red bell pepper, diced

This healthy meal is bursting with colour, flavour, and plenty of nutrition. It's also a quick and easy meal This recipe is a great example of how you can plan and pre-cook part of tomorrow's meal today. We used grilled chicken in the previous night's meal and fully cooked double the amount of chicken needed that night to include in this spaghetti dish the following evening. This dish could then easily be put together in little more time than it takes to bring the water to a boil and cook the pasta. We simply sliced the already cooked chicken breasts and warmed them quickly in the sauté pan with the rest of the ingredients before tossing together with the cooked spaghetti and serving. should have little problem getting on the table in about a half-hour or so.

1. Slice the chicken breasts against the grain and get the spaghetti boiling in lightly salted water.

2. In a large sauté pan, lightly sauté the garlic in the olive oil. Add the butter, the lemon juice and zest, oregano, white wine, and Dijon mustard. Simmer slowly for 1-2 minutes and then add asparagus and red pepper.

3. Cook for only 4-5 minutes until the asparagus is cooked but still has a little crispness. Add the sliced chicken in the last minute, just to warm it through. Pour the contents of the sauté pan over the cooked spaghetti and toss well before serving.

4. As a bonus, I've even served the leftovers as a cold pasta salad, and it's still delicious!

tip > One of the ways our family manages meal planning is to think ahead when cooking tonight and plan leftovers that can be turned into another meal. For example, I almost always grill double the amount of chicken breasts I need. They'll last a couple of days in the fridge and can be turned into panninis, chicken burgers, added in the last minute to stir-fried dishes, or just diced and added to pasta sauce we keep portioned and frozen in the freezer. A little imagination and planning is all it takes to make dinner faster and easier.

Dijon Chicken Linguine *with* Crimini Mushrooms and Toasted Almonds

SERVES 4

3 tbsp olive oil

4 boneless skinless chicken breasts

4 cloves garlic, minced

salt and pepper to season

4 oz white wine

2 cups whipping cream

3 tbsp Dijon mustard

1 cup sliced crimini mushrooms (you can also use button or chanterelle mushrooms)

350 g package fresh linguine, cooked

¼ cup toasted slivered almonds

It comes as no surprise to me that, even though *Rock Recipes* has over 1300 recipes published online since 2007, this dish is consistently in the top ten most popular recipes. I developed it after a similar restaurant dinner I had decades ago, and it's been requested by friends at countless dinner parties since. I think the simple flavours, ease of preparation, and luscious creamy sauce all attribute to its success. It's not only the website's second most popular chicken recipe but the most popular pasta recipe we've ever posted as well. This is one you'll make again and again.

1. Preheat oven to 200°F. Heat the olive oil in a large, heavy bottomed frying pan over medium-low heat. Add chicken breasts and garlic, and season with salt and pepper. Continue to fry the chicken until completely cooked. Remove chicken from pan and hold in the warm oven.

2. Add the white wine to the pan and simmer until volume is reduced by half.

3. Then add whipping cream, Dijon mustard, and salt and pepper to season. Simmer until sauce thickens enough to coat a metal spoon. Return chicken to the sauce, add the mushrooms and simmer for an additional 2 minutes. Serve over cooked linguine. Sprinkle with the toasted slivered almonds.

Super Quick Sesame Beef and Asparagus

SERVES 4

½ lb fresh asparagus

2 tbsp of peanut or regular sesame oil

1½ lbs thinly sliced steak

2 cloves garlic, minced

2 tsp freshly grated ginger root

3 tbsp oyster sauce (reduced-sodium version if available)

3 tbsp low-sodium soy sauce

1 tsp Chinese five-spice powder

3 tbsp rice wine vinegar

½ tsp black pepper

4 tbsp brown sugar

1 tbsp toasted sesame oil (more or less to taste)

1 tbsp cornstarch

¼ cup beef stock (or water)

3 tbsp toasted sesame seeds

¾ cup sliced water chestnuts

So how quick is super quick? Well, with good organization, I can have this on the table in about 20 minutes. I think good organization and time efficiency are really the keys to these sorts of recipes. For example, I always have two things going on simultaneously. While the water boils for blanching, chop the garlic and asparagus. While the asparagus blanches, slice the beef and grate the ginger. Always assemble all of the ingredients you will need on the counter next to the stove before you start cooking. You can even do that while waiting for the wok to heat.

1. Cut the asparagus into 1½-inch pieces and blanch in boiling salted water for only 3-4 minutes. Then drain the asparagus and immediately plunge it into ice water to stop the cooking and preserve its colour. (You can use broccoli or green beans here if you prefer, but use the same cooking method for them too.) After a minute, drain the ice water off the asparagus and set it aside.

2. Heat a wok over very high heat. Add 2 tbsp of peanut or regular sesame oil and quickly stir fry the steak slices for only 1-2 minutes. Remove the beef from the wok and set aside while you prepare the sauce.

3. To the wok, add the garlic, ginger, oyster sauce, soy sauce, five-spice powder, rice wine vinegar, black pepper, brown sugar, and toasted sesame oil. Bring to a boil for only a minute.

4. Dissolve the cornstarch in the beef stock (or water) and add to the simmering sauce in the wok, stirring constantly until the sauce thickens.

5. Add the beef back to the sauce along with the blanched asparagus and water chestnuts. Simmer only for another minute or so until the beef, water chestnuts, and asparagus are heated through. Serve over steamed rice or your favourite Chinese noodles.

6. Sprinkle on the toasted sesame seeds when serving.

Blueberry Balsamic Pork Chops

SERVES 4

8 boneless center-loin pork chops

salt and pepper to season

3 tbsp olive oil

2 cloves garlic, minced

1 cup blueberries, fresh or frozen

2 tbsp balsamic vinegar

½ cup white wine or chicken stock

½ tsp thyme

¼ tsp freshly grated nutmeg

1 tbsp brown sugar

2 tbsp honey

3 tbsp lemon juice

3 tbsp butter

Here's a bit of a different take on sweet and sour flavours in a simply prepared blueberry balsamic sauce, which gets served with pan-seared or grilled pork chops. They have become one of our family favourites and have been incredibly popular on my blog over the last couple of years too, gathering quite a number of rave reviews.

> **tip** > Concerns about undercooking pork are not what they were decades ago. Health Canada's recommended safe internal cooking temperature is now 160°F. This temperature will ensure fully cooked pork that hasn't lost its natural juiciness. Eliminate the guess work and worrying by always using a meat thermometer for all meat and poultry, and you'll know when your dish is cooked to perfection.

1. Preheat oven to 200°F. Season the pork chops with salt and pepper. Pan fry the pork chops in the olive oil and garlic until completely cooked, about 4-5 minutes per side. Hold the pork chops in the warm oven.

2. Add the blueberries, balsamic vinegar, wine (or stock), thyme, nutmeg, brown sugar, and honey. Simmer to reduce the volume of the sauce by half. Add the lemon juice and butter and simmer for an additional minute or so until the sauce slightly thickens. Season with salt and pepper to taste, and spoon the sauce over the cooked pork chops.

3. If your blueberries are particularly juicy (and especially when using frozen berries), you can thicken the sauce slightly, if necessary, by adding a slurry at the end made by dissolving together 1 tsp cornstarch and 1 oz water.

4. When using grilled pork chops instead of pan-fried, just begin the sauce by lightly sautéing the garlic then add the other ingredients as directed.

Sun-Dried Tomato Pesto Linguine

SERVES 6

½ cup whole unroasted almonds

2 cups oil-packed sun-dried tomatoes, drained

2 cloves garlic

¾ cup olive oil, or the oil the tomatoes were packed in.

1 tsp crushed chili paste (more or less to taste)

1 tsp freshly ground black pepper

4 tbsp chopped fresh chives (or other herb of your choice)

one 350g pkg fresh linguine

½ lemon, juiced

½ cup freshly grated Parmesan cheese

Here's one of my personal top ten recipes, not only for its deliciously complex flavours, but for its versatility too. I've been able to use this pesto in so many delicious ways I consider it one of my biggest recipe successes. Simply toss it with your favourite cooked pasta for a quick and easy workday meal that makes a great vegetarian dish too. You can add some simple grilled chicken or sautéed garlic shrimp to make it a more substantial meal for meat eaters, and these simple additions make it ideal to serve at a dinner party where you can serve it both ways.

1. Toast the almonds for about 10 minutes in a 350°F oven, tossing them once during that time. Then grind them in a food processor or blender until they are the consistency of a coarse cornmeal.

2. Add all the other ingredients to a blender or food processor. Process all together until almost smooth. Quickly pulse in the ground toasted almonds.

3. Cook the linguine in boiling salted water as directed on the package. Toss the cooked linguine with about 2½ cups of the pesto and some halved grape tomatoes if desired. Baby spinach leaves also make a nice addition when tossing together the pesto and pasta if you like. Serve immediately.

> **tip** > You can adjust the amount of oil in this pesto to suit your taste and purpose. Make it with less oil as a spread for crostini, or add it to strained yogurt for a delicious veggie dip; two great ideas for entertaining. If you make your own pasta, a thick version of this pesto also makes a delicious filling for ravioli, especially when served with Alfredo sauce. Use it in place of tomato sauce to make amazing homemade pizza too.

The Best Beef and Broccoli

SERVES 4

1½ lbs of broccoli, cleaned and cut into 1½-inch florets

1½ lbs strip loin steak, thick cut to 1½ inches

2 tbsp peanut oil

salt and pepper to season

2 cloves garlic, minced

¼ tsp freshly ground nutmeg

½ tsp Chinese five-spice powder

½ tsp fresh grated ginger

4 tbsp hoisin sauce

2 tbsp oyster sauce

⅔ cup beef stock

cornstarch slurry (1 tbsp cornstarch dissolved in 3 tbsp cold water)

1 tsp toasted sesame oil

This Chinese take-out favourite makes a terrific quick-cooked meal for a busy weekday or busier weekend supper. We serve it with steamed rice or, even more often, Chinese noodles. It's one sure way to get my kids to eat their broccoli.

1. Steam the broccoli florets for only about 3 to 4 minutes. Drop the steamed florets into a big bowl of ice water to stop the cooking action. Drain the florets from the cold water and set aside.

2. Slice the beef across the grain in thin slices. Heat the peanut oil in a wok at the highest heat. Lightly season the beef strips with salt and pepper and cook the beef strips in small batches for only a couple of minutes in the wok. Set aside.

3. Sauté the minced garlic in the wok for a minute before adding the freshly ground nutmeg, five-spice powder, ginger, hoisin sauce, oyster sauce, and beef stock. Simmer together for a few minutes before adding enough of the cornstarch slurry to thicken the sauce. Taste the sauce and do a final seasoning with salt and pepper if necessary. Then add the toasted sesame oil.

4. Toss the cooked beef strips and broccoli back into the sauce and toss together over high heat only for a minute until the broccoli is heated through. Serve over rice or Chinese noodles. Toasted cashews make a nice garnish too.

Spicy Mango Orange Pork and Cashews

SERVES 4

3 tbsp peanut oil

2 cloves garlic, minced

1 lb thinly sliced pork tenderloin

salt and pepper to season

1 cup diced red bell pepper

1 cup orange juice

4 tbsp hoisin sauce

4 tbsp rice wine or Chinese cooking wine

3 tbsp rice wine vinegar (or apple cider vinegar in a pinch)

3 tbsp honey

1 tsp crushed chili sauce or ½ tsp chili flakes (optional or to taste)

2 tsp soya sauce

2 tsp toasted sesame oil

½ tsp Chinese five-spice powder

1 tbsp finely grated fresh ginger

1 tsp cornstarch dissolved in 1 oz of cold water

2 fresh mangoes, diced

¾ cup toasted cashews

⅓ cup chopped green onions

This is my kind of quick and easy family dinner. Although, I will also confess that, when on the rare occasion I'm left alone for dinner, I can whip up a single serving of this in no time flat. On those occasions, I will most likely very thinly slice a single pork chop to use in this dish rather than the pork tenderloin. As long as it's quickly cooked, it works almost as well as the more tender loin meat.

We serve this most often over thin Chinese noodles, which cook in just a few minutes, but it's also terrific with plain steamed rice too. This dish comes together so quickly your family could be sitting down to dinner in less time than it takes for a take-out delivery…and it's likely to be a whole lot tastier too.

1. Heat peanut oil in a wok over high heat. Quickly add the garlic and pork, season with salt and pepper, and stir fry for only about a minute. Add the peppers and stir fry for only about another 30 seconds. Remove the pork and peppers from the wok and set aside.

2. To the wok add the orange juice, and simmer to reduce the juice volume by half before adding, all at once, the hoisin sauce, Chinese cooking wine, rice wine vinegar, honey, crushed chili sauce, soya sauce, toasted sesame oil, Chinese five-spice powder, and fresh ginger.

3. Simmer for a couple of minutes before returning the pork and peppers to the wok with the sauce. Bring to a boil and thicken with the slurry of cornstarch dissolved in an ounce of cold water.

4. Toss in the diced fresh mangoes, and cook for only a minute to warm through the mango. Serve over noodles or rice, and when serving, sprinkle the plates with toasted cashews and chopped green onions.

Shrimp and Egg Fried Quinoa

SERVES 4

1 cup quinoa

2 cups chicken stock (or water)

2 dozen large shrimp

2 tbsp + 2 tbsp peanut oil

salt and pepper to season

2 cloves garlic, minced

½ cup finely diced red onion

2 tsp toasted sesame oil

3 beaten eggs

½ cup chopped red bell pepper

1 tsp chili flakes (or 2 tsp crushed chili paste), more or less to taste

1 tsp grated fresh ginger

1 tsp Chinese five-spice powder

Quinoa recipes seem to be everywhere these days, and Spouse was one of the early converts to this super-food trend. I have to admit, I love its nutty flavour too. I'm not a big rice fan, so I always welcome a tasty alternative. Quinoa is actually a seed and not a grain and has been cultivated for thousands of years. It's high protein, low-fat, gluten free, and is also high in essential minerals like iron and magnesium, so when a tasty alternative to rice comes packing that kind of nutritional power, you can see why our family has made it a part of our menu planning.

1. Slowly simmer together the quinoa and chicken stock with a pinch of salt for about 20 minutes, until the quinoa is fully cooked and tender. Don't overcook it to mushy; it should still have a little bite to it. When cooked, spread the quinoa out in a shallow baking dish or on a parchment-lined baking sheet to cool quickly. This helps preserve the texture of the quinoa. It doesn't need to be cold, just let it steam off. You can also have your quinoa cooked and cooled in advance and just pull it out of the fridge to use in this recipe at dinner time for an easy meal in minutes. While the quinoa cooks, you can prepare the other components of the dish.

2. Lightly sauté the shrimp in 2 tbsp peanut oil, with salt and pepper to taste. Drain the shrimp on paper towels and set them aside until later.

3. In a wok or large nonstick sauté pan over medium-heat, add the minced garlic, diced red onion, 2 tbsp peanut oil, and 2 tsp toasted sesame oil. Cook for only a minute or so until the onions soften, then add the eggs and chopped red pepper.

4. Cook the eggs to a hard scramble, chopping them into small pieces. Turn the heat up to medium-high and add the cooled quinoa and sautéed shrimp along with the chili flakes, ginger, and five-spice powder.

5. Toss together in the wok and stir fry for 2-3 minutes before serving. Garnish with a sprinkle of fresh chopped green onions.

Quick and Easy Kung Pao Chicken

SERVES 4

4 boneless skinless chicken breasts, cut in small cubes

4 cloves garlic, minced

pinch + ½ tsp fresh ground black pepper

2 tbsp peanut oil

a few dried Szechuan chili peppers (or use Chinese chili paste to taste)

¼ cup rice wine

2 tbsp hoisin sauce

2 tbsp black bean sauce

3 tbsp sugar

1 tbsp fresh grated ginger root

½ tsp Chinese five-spice powder

1 tsp toasted sesame oil

2 tbsp light soy sauce

1 tbsp dark soy sauce

1 red bell pepper, diced

4 green onions, chopped in 1-inch pieces

cornstarch slurry (1 oz water and 1 tsp cornstarch)

toasted peanuts or cashews

Kung Pao Chicken has long been one of my favourite take-out lunches, especially when I crave something spicy. I played around with quite a number of recipes to come up with this simple but very flavourful homemade version that I think stacks up quite well against some restaurant versions.

It's also one of the recipes I regularly make if only one or two family members are home for dinner because most of the ingredients are those that we always have on hand for Asian cooking and because I can have it on the table in minutes.

1. In a hot wok, sauté the chicken with the garlic and a pinch of pepper until almost completely cooked. Remove the chicken from the wok for the time being.

2. To the hot wok, add the peanut oil and Szechuan chili peppers (you can substitute Chinese chili paste to better control the heat to your taste. Start with about a teaspoon for mild heat). Toss the chili peppers in the oil for a few seconds before adding all the following ingredients quickly and all at once: rice wine, hoisin sauce, black bean sauce, sugar, grated ginger root, Chinese five-spice powder, toasted sesame oil, light soy sauce, dark soy sauce, and ½ tsp freshly ground black pepper.

3. Reduce the heat on the wok to medium and bring the sauce to a simmer before adding the chicken back to the wok. Then add diced red pepper and chopped green onions.

4. Cook for an additional minute. To thicken the sauce, stir in a slurry of 1 oz water and 1 tsp cornstarch.

5. Serve on a bed of rice or Chinese noodles and garnish with toasted peanuts or cashews.

4 large boneless, skinless chicken breasts cut in thick strips (about 4 or 5 per breast)

1 cup flour

½ tsp black pepper

¼ tsp cayenne pepper

1 tbsp ground ginger

½ tsp ground nutmeg

1 tsp salt

1 egg + 2 tbsp water, whisked to make an egg wash

3 tbsp peanut oil

3 cloves garlic, minced

2 cups orange juice

½ cup hoisin sauce

4 tbsp rice wine or Chinese cooking wine

3 tbsp rice wine vinegar (or apple cider vinegar in a pinch)

6 tbsp brown sugar

2 tsp chili paste (optional or to taste or use chili flakes to taste)

4 tsp soya sauce

2 tsp toasted sesame oil

cornstarch slurry (2 tsp cornstarch dissolved in ¼ cup cold water)

1 red bell pepper, diced

1 cup sliced button mushrooms (optional)

1 cup steamed snow peas

Baked Orange Hoisin Chicken

In another of our baked and not fried Chinese meal options, this delicious chicken takes mere minutes to bake to a crispy golden brown in a hot oven before being tossed in a delicious and easy to make orange hoisin sauce. It's important to heat the pan in the oven first to make sure the chicken gets crispy in the short cooking time. This recipe's great served over Chinese noodles or rice for a delicious meal in about 30 minutes.

> tip > Whenever adapting a flour and spice coated chicken recipe from fried to baked—whether it's full, bone-in chicken pieces or just chicken nuggets for the kids—a spray bottle is a useful tool to help control the amount of oil used. My method is to brush the pan with oil, add the chicken pieces, then lightly spray them with oil before popping them into a hot oven. Turning the chicken pieces halfway through the cooking time helps make them evenly crunchy on all sides too.

1. Preheat oven to 425°F, and warm a baking pan in the oven.

2. Combine the flour, black pepper, cayenne pepper, ground ginger, ground nutmeg, and salt.

3. Dip the chicken pieces in the flour mixture, then in the egg wash, then dredge them again in the flour mixture. Place on a lightly oiled baking sheet and lightly drizzle over the tops with a little more peanut oil. Bake in the 425° oven for about 20 minutes. Flip the pieces halfway through the cooking time. While the chicken is baking, prepare your sauce.

4. Heat 3 tbsp of peanut oil in a wok over medium-high heat. Quickly add the minced garlic and stir fry for only about a minute. Then to the wok add the orange juice.

5. Simmer to reduce the orange juice volume by half before adding, all at once, the hoisin sauce, rice wine, rice wine vinegar, brown sugar, chili paste (optional), soya sauce, and toasted sesame oil.

6. Bring to a boil and thicken with a slurry of 2 tsp cornstarch dissolved in ¼ cup cold water. Toss in the diced red pepper, sliced button mushrooms (optional), and steamed snow peas.

7. Toss in the baked chicken pieces. Serve over rice or Chinese noodles.

Slow-Cooked Sunday is not only about what's in the oven or on the stove top; it's about taking the time to slow down while something simmers away or slowly braises for hours with the promise of great comfort food at the end of the day. Whether it's more practical for you to do so on a Saturday or a Sunday, the weekend is meant to be a time for your family, big or small, to re-energize and reconnect after a long, busy week, and what better way to regenerate than a soul restoring family meal? Many of these recipes need very little attention after their initial preparation, so you can take some time to relax while dinner gradually takes care of itself. Isn't that what a weekend day off should be all about?

Slow-Cooked Sundays

Maple Pulled Pork and Beans

SERVES 10

1 lb dry white beans, pre-soaked overnight

3 lbs pork shoulder or butt

1 tsp powdered ginger

1 tsp black pepper

½ tsp ground cumin

1 tsp chili powder

½ tsp salt

3 tbsp canola oil

½ lb smoked bacon, cut in small pieces

1 large white onion, chopped

3 cloves garlic, minced

2 cups water

2 tsp freshly ground black pepper

2 tsp chipotle powder (more or less to taste)

1 tsp salt

½ cup brown sugar

½ cup apple cider vinegar

1½ tsp dry thyme

4 cups pureed canned tomatoes

1 cup maple syrup

3 large bay leaves

On a cold, rainy Sunday a while back, I decided a slow-cooking day was in order. How better to ignore the torrent of rain outside than to sit back and watch old movies all afternoon while supper languidly bubbles away in the oven for several hours, needing very little attention at all.

On days like that, my son usually requests one of his two slow-cooked favourites, either baked beans or pulled pork. Since pork and beans is a natural combination I decided to try combining the two. Needless to say, the boy was very pleased.

> tip > You will need to pre-soak the beans in water at least overnight. The longer you soak the beans the less time it takes to cook them, although it will still be several hours. I have soaked beans for up to 48 hours in advance.

1. Preheat the oven to 325°F. Cut the pork into about ½ to 2-inch cubes. Mix together the ginger, pepper, cumin, chili powder, and salt to form a rub for the pork. Rub it into the cubed pork. Heat the canola oil in the bottom of a large Dutch oven over medium to medium-high heat. Add the seasoned pork cubes and brown them well. Remove from the pot and set aside.

2. Add the bacon to the pot and cook until almost crispy. Drain excess fat. Add the onion and minced garlic and cook until softened.

3. Drain the beans from the water they were soaked in and add them to the pot. Add all of the remaining ingredients to the pot. If your Dutch oven is not large enough, you can transfer everything to a large covered roaster. Stir all together well, cover, and place in the preheated oven for 3-4 hours, stirring occasionally.

4. The beans should be fully cooked and tender, and the sauce should thicken. I sometimes add a little extra boiling water during the cooking time if the sauce thickens too quickly before the beans are fully cooked. This is not a problem at all and can be done more than once if necessary.

4-5 lb beef roast (blade or cross-rib cuts work well)

canola oil

salt and pepper to season

4 oz pancetta, finely diced (or bacon)

3 tbsp olive oil

2 carrots, diced small

3 celery stalks, diced small

4 cloves garlic, minced

2 large onions, finely diced

4 cups crushed canned tomatoes

3 cups beef stock

2 cups red wine

1 tsp freshly grated nutmeg

2 bay leaves

leftover suggestions >

- Pull the beef into pieces, toss in a little of the sauce, and serve on toasted crusty bread with melting provolone cheese.

- Serve pulled beef and sauce tossed with pasta and served with grated Parmesan cheese.

Pot Roast Bolognese

Everyone loves a good pasta Bolognese, right? This is a great weekend cooking idea because you can make a very large pot roast and have leftovers for a meal or two in the early days of the week ahead. We served this pot roast with some roasted potatoes and steamed vegetables on Sunday, then enjoyed pulled beef Bolognese sandwiches with melted provolone the next day. The remaining pulled beef and sauce was then simply warmed and served over pasta the next day; one relaxing slow-cooking Sunday, three days of incredibly delicious meals...what's better than that?

Substituting ground beef or an even combination of beef, veal, and pork will also make my recipe for Basic Bolognese Sauce, which I very slowly simmer over low heat for several hours. Since it is a large batch, leftover sauce can be frozen in airtight containers and thawed for much appreciated slow-cooked flavour in a quick workday meal served with your favourite pasta.

1. Preheat oven to 325°F. Season the roast with salt and pepper and brown on all sides in a cast-iron pan with a little canola oil added to the pan. Transfer the roast to a covered roaster or heavy Dutch oven. To the frying pan add the finely diced pancetta.

2. Cook over medium heat until the pancetta renders its fat and begins to brown. Then add the olive oil, diced carrots, diced celery, minced garlic, diced onion, and salt and pepper to season. Cook until the onions have softened but not browned.

3. Add the vegetable mixture to the roasting pan along with the tomatoes, beef stock, red wine, grated nutmeg, and bay leaves. Cover and place in the preheated oven for 2-3 hours until the meat is fall-apart tender.

4. Serve with roasted potatoes and steamed vegetables.

Brown Sugar and Dijon Glazed Ham

Now Spouse loves her ham and, if allowed, would chuck the turkey in favour of this sweet and savoury glazed ham at any holiday celebration. A Sunday ham is a terrific choice because of all the leftover possibilities, or just cook one to "pick on" as my mother's family would say, meaning to have one on hand in the fridge for a quick lunch with a simple salad, for ham sandwiches, ham and eggs, or just a succulent sliver all on its own.

We very rarely make another ham recipe at our house for sheer fear of the disappointment that it will not live up to the standard set by this outstanding recipe.

7-8 lb bone in smoked ham

2 tbsp pepper corns

1 tbsp whole cloves

1 whole star anise

1 large onion, roughly chopped

1 bay leaf

whole-grain Dijon mustard

about ⅔ cup brown sugar

1. Add the pepper corns, cloves, star anise, onion, and bay leaf to a large stock pot along with the ham, rind side down, and cover almost completely with water. Bring to a gentle boil and cook for 1 hour.

2. After an hour, remove the ham from the stock and let it drain on a rack for a few minutes. Preheat the oven to 375°F. Remove the rind from the ham and most but not all of the fat underneath the rind. Leave about ⅛-inch of fat on top of the entire ham. Score the fat with a sharp knife in a square or diamond pattern. Leave the ham to cool for 10 minutes then dry the exterior with paper towels.

3. Place ham in a roasting pan and brush the top and sides of the ham with whole-grain Dijon mustard, and sprinkle generously with brown sugar.

4. Press the sugar gently into the mustard to get good contact with the surface of the ham.

Bake in the preheated oven for another hour, basting the ham several times during roasting.

5. Allow ham to rest for 10-15 minutes before carving and serving.

Herb and Garlic-Crusted Prime-Rib Roast *with* Burgundy Thyme Gravy

SERVES 6–8

HERB AND GARLIC-CRUSTED PRIME-RIB ROAST

4½-5 lb prime-rib roast

6 cloves garlic, minced

1 tsp kosher salt

1 tsp cracked black pepper

3-4 tbsp Dijon mustard

½ cup fresh chopped mixed herbs (oregano, rosemary, and thyme work well)

BURGUNDY THYME GRAVY

4 cups beef broth (or a combination of fat skimmed pan drippings and beef broth to make 4 cups)

1 cup burgundy wine

4 sprigs fresh thyme (or about 1 tsp dried ground thyme)

¼ cup butter

¼ cup flour

½ tsp freshly ground black pepper

2 cloves garlic, minced

This is one of my favourite celebration meals, and although I do cook prime-rib roast several ways, this is still the easiest and one of the most flavourful. The burgundy thyme gravy is something I almost always serve with this particular meal along with roasted garlic mashed potatoes and roasted root vegetables. Some Perfect Popovers (see recipe on page 190) are also almost essential with this meal, at least in our family.

> **tip** > A Sunday roast dinner is a good opportunity for a reminder about the importance of letting any roasted meat rest before carving. Coming out of a hot oven, the molecules in the natural meat juices are moving very fast and will seep out very quickly if carved right away. Instead allow 15-20 minutes, even longer for large roasts, for the meat to cool slightly, relax, and settle back in its own juices. It really does make a world of difference, even to the leftovers.

HERB AND GARLIC-CRUSTED PRIME-RIB ROAST

1.   Preheat oven to 375°F. Mix together the 6 cloves of minced garlic, kosher salt, cracked black pepper, Dijon mustard, and mixed herbs.

2.   Rub the herb-garlic mix all over the surface of the roast. Press it into the meat a little to make it stick as much as possible. Place the roast, rib side down, uncovered on a rack in the preheated oven until the center reaches the desired temperature on a meat thermometer: 145°F for rare, 160° to 165°F for medium, and 175° to 180°F for well done.

3. It's essential that you let the roast rest, tented in aluminum foil, for about 20 minutes for a large roast. This allows the juices to settle and the meat fibers to relax, making the meat far more tender.

BURGUNDY THYME GRAVY

1. Simmer together the beef broth, burgundy wine, and fresh thyme uncovered for about 20-30 minutes until the volume of the liquid is reduced by about one third.

2. In a separate heavy bottomed saucepan add the butter, flour, ground black pepper, and 2 cloves minced garlic.

3. Cook together, stirring constantly, for 2-3 minutes until foamy. Slowly and steadily whisk in the boiling broth mixture. Whisk quickly and steadily as you add the hot liquid to prevent lumps in the gravy. Season with salt to taste. Add a little more beef broth if you like thinner gravy.

ST. JOHN'S STOUT STEW

4 lbs beef, cut in 1½ inch cubes

plain flour for dredging

24 oz Yellowbelly St. John's Stout Beer (Guinness makes a fine substitute)

8 cups good beef stock (if not using homemade, choose a good quality brand, low-sodium stock)

8 slices bacon, crisp cooked and crumbled

1 cup orange juice

1 whole nutmeg, grated

2 tsp cracked black pepper

3 sprigs fresh rosemary, chopped

4 tbsp fresh thyme

½ tsp ground cloves

6 cloves garlic, chopped

2 small red onions, minced

2 lbs carrots, cut in coins or sticks

1 lb parsnip, cut in large chunks

1 lb turnip, cut in large chunks

1 lb pearl onions

olive oil

2 lbs of fingerling or other baby yellow or red potatoes

2-3 cups button mushrooms

WHOLE-WHEAT IRISH SODA BREAD

3 cups soft whole-wheat flour

1 cup soft white flour (cake flour works well)

1½ tsp baking soda

1¾ cups buttermilk

St. John's Stout Stew *with* Whole-Wheat Irish Soda Bread

Cooking a great stew is a process of building layers of flavour which meld together to form a dish much greater than the sum of its parts, and this one is no exception. The layers of flavour begin with the beef, which is dredged in flour before browning. The flour not only aids in browning the beef but also helps thicken the stew's rich gravy. The beef is then slowly braised in a local microbrewery stout beer, beef stock, a little orange juice, garlic, onions, spices, and fresh herbs until it's melt-in-your-mouth tender.

Fantastic locally sourced vegetables are a must in a stew of this caliber. The vegetables are roasted to caramelize them a little and bring out their natural sweetness before adding them to the stew, providing yet another layer of flavour to the pot. Finally, potatoes, sweet pearl onions, and earthy mushrooms help to finish this rich, balanced, and oh so comforting stew.

ST. JOHN'S STOUT STEW

1. Preheat oven to 350°F. Season the beef with salt and pepper then dredge the cubes in plain flour before browning them in some canola oil in a large frying pan. Work in small batches so as not to crowd the pan. This will make browning the beef easier. Transfer the cooked beef to a large covered roasting pan or large Dutch oven. I often use a large enamel-covered turkey roaster.

2. To the roasting pan add the stout, beef stock, crumbled bacon, orange juice, nutmeg, cracked black pepper, rosemary, thyme, ground cloves, chopped garlic, and red onions. Place the covered roaster in the preheated oven for about 2 hours.

3. Meanwhile, peel, wash, and cut the carrots, parsnip, turnip, and pearl onions.

4. Toss the vegetables in a little olive oil, pepper, and sea salt. Place them on a cookie sheet and roast on the lower rack in the oven for about 40 minutes. You do not have to remove the beef while the vegetables roast.

5. Add the roasted vegetables to the slow-cooked beef along with the potatoes. Return to the oven for about another 30 to 40 minutes or until the potatoes are fork tender. In the last 10 minutes of cooking time add the button mushrooms.

WHOLE-WHEAT IRISH SODA BREAD

1. Preheat oven to 425°F.

2. Sift together whole-wheat flour, soft white flour, and baking soda. Form a well in the middle of the dry ingredients and pour in the buttermilk. Mix together with a wooden spoon only until a soft dough forms and the flour is fully incorporated. Turn the dough out onto a floured surface and form into a 10-inch round. Place on a parchment-lined baking sheet. Using a sharp knife, cut an X into the surface of the dough about a half-inch deep and reaching to about an inch from the edge of the dough.

3. Bake for 30-35 minutes until golden brown and crusty and sounds hollow when tapped.

French Onion Braised Beef Brisket

Beef brisket does take a long time to slowly cook to tender perfection, but it's so worth the wait. Brisket has some of the best flavour of any cut of beef, so there's a reward for your effort. I don't really consider slow-cooked meals to be as much work as some folks do. Once the initial preparation is done and the brisket's in the oven, it's just a matter of time and not work. So if you're at home all afternoon anyway, what's the big deal?

Other cuts of beef suitable for braising—like chuck, bottom round, blade roast, or even flank steak—will work well in this recipe and can shave at least an hour off the cooking time, depending on their size. Taking the time to slowly caramelize the onions is of paramount importance in this recipe; it's the flavour base of the entire dish and shouldn't be rushed. And remember: once that part's done and it's in the oven, you really just coast through the next few hours until it's time to serve up this fantastic comfort-food dinner.

SERVES 6–8

4-5 lb beef brisket

3 large onions, white or red, sliced thin

2 tbsp butter

salt and pepper to season

canola oil

2 cloves garlic, minced

1 quart/litre low-sodium beef stock

1 cup red wine

2 bay leaves

2 tbsp chopped fresh thyme (or 2 tsp dry thyme)

fresh ground nutmeg

3 tbsp Worcestershire sauce

1. Begin by caramelizing the onions. Add the butter to a sauté pan along with the onions and garlic over medium heat. Season with salt and pepper. Slowly cook the onions until they are softened and begin to slowly caramelize and turn brown. Do not do this too quickly, or they'll develop a bitter flavour. Slow cooking the onions will bring out their natural sweetness. Don't rush this. It will take 15-20 minutes or so.

2. Preheat your oven to 325°F. In a cast-iron pan over medium-high heat, add a little canola oil. Season the brisket with salt and pepper, and brown the brisket on all sides before adding it to a covered roasting pan. To the roasting pan, add all the other ingredients, including the caramelized onions. Season with salt and pepper.

3. Cover the roasting pan with aluminum foil as tightly as possible before adding the lid. Place in the preheated oven for 4 hours or until the brisket is fall-apart tender. Skim the excess fat from the pan drippings and serve as a jus with the brisket, or use it to make a gravy, whichever you prefer.

leftover suggestions >

- Serve with Perfect Popovers (recipe on page 190), and make additional popovers for an amazing stuffed brisket sandwich with the French onion braising liquid as an au jus dip. Leftovers were never more satisfying or delicious than this.

Orange Clove Brined Roast Turkey

SERVES 10–12
(WITH LEFTOVERS)

BRINE MIXTURE

You'll need a food-grade plastic bucket or large pan, big enough to completely submerge the turkey in the brine, for this recipe.

6 quarts or liters of water
(a little more if needed to cover the turkey completely)

⅓ cup table salt

½ cup sugar

¼ cup honey

8 whole cloves

1 large onion, sliced

3 cloves garlic, sliced thin

zest and juice of 2 large oranges

3 tbsp whole black peppercorns

ORANGE CLOVE BRINED
ROAST TURKEY

10-12 lb fresh turkey

2 tbsp of butter

1 onion quartered

2 cloves garlic, sliced

1 whole orange, punctured with a fork several times

melted butter for basting

If you have never brined a turkey before, it's time to learn what a delicious difference it can make. I'm partial to a flavour infused, brined turkey for maximum taste and juiciness in a roast turkey recipe. This one relies on just a few simple ingredients in the brine mixture to impart subtle hints of citrus and spice to the turkey meat. This is best done overnight, but a minimum of 6-8 hours in the brine will be required for the turkey, so plan well in advance for this recipe. For a little extra citrus boost, I roast the turkey with an orange stuffed into the cavity along with some onions and garlic. This recipe does not overwhelm the natural flavour of the turkey at all but gently compliments it with aromatic scent and flavour.

1. In a bucket, combine the water, table salt, sugar, and honey, stirring well to completely dissolve the sugar and salt. Then add the cloves, onion, garlic, orange juice and zest, and black peppercorns.

2. Wash the turkey well and completely submerge it in the bucket of brine. A plate with a couple of heavy cans of tomatoes or beans placed over the turkey will help keep it submerged. Place in the refrigerator overnight or for at least 6-8 hours. I remove one of the shelves in the fridge to make space for the bucket.

3. After brining the turkey, remove it from the brine and pat it dry with paper towels. Preheat the oven to 400°F. Place the turkey on a rack in a roasting pan and truss the turkey with butcher twine (or just tuck the wing tips under the turkey and tie the legs together to simplify things). There's no need to add additional salt or pepper, the brine has already seasoned the meat throughout. Rub the surface of the turkey with a couple of tablespoons of butter. To the cavity add the quartered onion, sliced garlic, and the whole orange.

tip > Although it's traditional in Newfoundland cooking to roast a turkey in a covered roaster, this is a sure way to ensure a dry, overcooked turkey. I *never* roast a turkey covered, always leaving it to open roast in the oven. This crisps the skin and seals in the natural juices, creating a turkey basted in its own juices. And I *always* use a meat thermometer to test if the turkey is cooked. Open roasting, getting the meat to 185°F, and properly resting the turkey before carving is the best way to prepare a juicy succulent turkey. If you don't own a meat thermometer, you should. It is the safest way to ensure poultry is fully cooked and very useful for getting that perfect medium-rare prime rib roast beef too; it's a kitchen essential for sure.

4. Do not cover the turkey. Open roast the turkey in the preheated oven for 30 minutes before reducing the temperature to 350°F. Brush the turkey with melted butter about every 30-45 minutes to get a nicely browned skin. After reducing the heat, continue roasting for about an additional 2 hours or until the internal temperature of the thickest part of the breast meat reaches 185°F on a meat thermometer. This could be more or less time depending on the actual size of the turkey you're roasting. Using a meat thermometer is the best way to make sure your turkey is completely and safely cooked. Remove from oven and cover with aluminum foil and allow the turkey to rest for 20 minutes before carving.

5. After the turkey has rested, I still make gravy from the pan drippings and the frozen turkey stock I *always* have on hand, made from the carcass of my last roast turkey. I *always* use stock and not water to make the best gravy. Low-sodium or no-salt-added, store-bought turkey or chicken stock are also good options if you don't have your own homemade stock available, but be sure to make some from the remnants of this turkey and freeze in plastic containers for soup or to make the most delicious turkey gravy next time. I still thicken my gravy the way my grandmother did with a slurry of flour and water, about a ½ cup of flour with just enough water to make the consistency of a very thin batter with no lumps. My grandmother always did it by shaking the slurry in an old jam jar. Add the slurry to the stock a little at a time and bring the gravy back to a boil after each addition. Use only enough of the flour slurry to achieve the consistency of gravy that you like. I always prefer it on the thinner side.

PINK PEPPERCORN PICKLED ONIONS

1 large red onion, sliced

3 tbsp pink peppercorns

¾ cup apple cider vinegar

3 tbsp brown sugar

¼ cup water

¼ tsp salt

2 tbsp black peppercorns
(optional, use only if you love
strong peppery flavour)

APPLE BRAISED PULLED CHICKEN

6-7 lb stewing hen

½ tsp powdered ginger

1 tsp cumin

1 tbsp + 1 tsp freshly ground
black pepper

1 tbsp dry thyme

1 tbsp garlic powder

1 tbsp dry oregano

1½ tbsp kosher salt

2 medium-sized onions, chopped

5-6 medium-sized firm apples,
peeled and chunked

½ cup brown sugar

½ cup molasses

¼ cup Worcestershire sauce

¼ cup Dijon mustard

½ cup apple cider vinegar

3 or more tbsp hot sauce (adjust
to taste)

1½ tsp salt

1 tsp freshly ground black pepper

1 cup apple juice

1 tsp powdered ginger

1 tsp Chinese five-spice powder

2 tbsp smoked paprika

Apple Braised Pulled Chicken Sandwiches *with* Pink Peppercorn Pickled Onions

This recipe was a challenge put forth by Spouse when she once found large stewing chickens on sale at the market. I'm not a particular fan of these larger, tougher chickens, but I have to say this tweaking of my pulled pork recipe was a delicious and very economical dinner. We served it over a couple of days to family and friends, and they all loved it.

The Pink Peppercorn Pickled Onions were delicious on this sandwich too. This is a quick pickling method meant to be used within a week or two of preparation but can be traditionally pickled in sealed and sterilized jars using the recommended method to last much longer. It is a great condiment for sausages, hot dogs, hamburgers, and even cold baked ham.

PINK PEPPERCORN PICKLED RED ONIONS

1. Layer the sliced onions alternately with a sprinkle of pink peppercorns in a jar. Stuff as many onions in the jar as you can. Bring the other ingredients just to a boil then pour over the onions and peppercorns. Carefully put the lid on and let sit for at least 24 hours.

APPLE BRAISED PULLED CHICKEN

1. Remove all the skin from the stewing hen and cut it into 8 pieces: two wings, two thighs, two breast halves, and two drumsticks.

tip > When making slow cooked or braised recipes that take several hours, I use any additional oven space to make beef or chicken stock as well, saving money, energy, and time. I save beef and chicken bones in my freezer then roast them off in a Dutch oven with chunks of onion, carrot, celery and a few garlic cloves for about 45 minutes. Then I cover them with water, replace the lid, and return to the oven for at least a couple of hours. I then strain it and freeze it in 16oz plastic containers for soups, gravies, and sauces when needed.

2. Combine the ginger, cumin, ground black pepper, thyme, garlic powder, oregano, and kosher salt, and rub all over the surface of the chicken pieces. (You can do this step the day before and let the chicken marinate in the spices overnight, if you like, to really infuse the flavour into the chicken.) Brown the chicken pieces in a little oil in a cast-iron skillet for just a few minutes on each side. They do not need to be fully cooked in this browning process.

3. Transfer the browned chicken pieces to a covered roasting pan. To the roasting pan, along with the chicken, add the chopped onion and chunked apples.

4. Preheat oven to 300°F. Meanwhile, in a medium-size bowl, mix the brown sugar, molasses, Worcestershire sauce, Dijon mustard, apple cider vinegar, hot sauce, salt, black pepper, apple juice, ginger, Chinese five-spice powder, and smoked paprika. Pour all over the chicken, apples, and onions in the roasting pan. Cover with aluminum foil then the lid of the roasting pan. Roast in the preheated oven for about 3 hours, until the meat is very tender and falling off the bones.

5. Remove the braising liquid to a saucepan, skim all the excess fat, and reduce the liquid until it slightly thickens. At this point you can puree the sauce with an immersion blender or in a food processor to smooth it out and incorporate the cooked onions and apples.

6. Remove the chicken from the bones and pull it into small pieces. Pour the sauce back over the shredded chicken and toss well to coat the chicken pieces in the sauce.

7. Serve on toasted bread with the pickled onions. We made our sandwiches with toasted artisan bread from our neighbourhood Georgestown Bakery, but use any good quality bread you like. This great sandwich really deserves great bread.

8. Simply substituting a pork butt or shoulder roast, instead of chicken, makes excellent pulled pork as well.

Tomato Braised Leg of Lamb
with Spinach Feta Stuffing

SERVES 6–8

4-5 lb boneless leg of lamb

SPINACH FETA AND PINE NUT STUFFING

1 small red onion, chopped

2 cloves garlic, minced

3 tbsp olive oil

3 cups good crusty bread, toasted

2 tbsp chopped fresh oregano (or 1 tbsp dried oregano)

⅓ cup crumbled feta cheese

1 cup chopped spinach

pinch of salt

pinch of black pepper

⅔ cup veal or beef stock

1 egg

TOMATO BRAISING SAUCE

3 cloves garlic, minced

4 cups chopped canned San Marzano Tomatoes (or plum tomatoes)

2 tbsp balsamic vinegar

1 tbsp brown sugar

salt and pepper to season

2 tbsp chopped fresh oregano (or 1 tbsp dried oregano)

1½ cups veal or beef stock

Leg of lamb is a real treat for me because I rarely make it at home. I love lamb, but a single rack for one is usually how I have to enjoy it since it's one of the few dinner menu sticking points for the rest of the family. I blame Spouse for some of this. Her late father, Len, had a distaste for lamb and used what we'll call a "colourful phrase" for declaring it unfit to eat. He, of course, found it quite humorous, but it seems to have had a lasting effect.

I'm slowly winning the rest of the family over though, and this new recipe was my greatest success to date. They all love the Mediterranean flavours of Greece, where lamb is such a culinary staple, so I started there and threw in a little Italian for good measure with the famous canned San Marzano tomatoes that are the base for many sauces at our house, including the best pizza sauce ever. These tomatoes are the key ingredient in this tender braised lamb recipe.

> **tip** > Grown in the volcanic ash enriched soil near Mt. Vesuvius, there's something almost intangibly magic about the flavour of San Marzano tomatoes: not too acidic and retaining much more of their natural fresh flavour when canned, they really can't be bested. Use them if you can get them.

SPINACH FETA AND PINE NUT STUFFING

1. Sauté the onion and garlic in the olive oil until softened, then add them to a large bowl along with the bread, oregano, feta cheese, spinach, salt and pepper, and toss together well.

2. Whisk together the stock and the egg. Pour over the stuffing and toss well. Let stand a few minutes, occasionally pressing down on the bread cubes to ensure they absorb all of the liquid.

3. Set the leg of lamb on a cutting board, cover with plastic wrap, and pound flat with a meat mallet to about 1 to 1½-inch thickness. Place the stuffing evenly along the center line of the flattened roast. Bring the sides of the roast up over the stuffing and tie with several lengths of butcher string to close. I usually use a couple of lengths of butcher string to tie the two ends closed as well so they cross the other strings at a 90 degree angle.

4. Season the outside of the roast with salt and pepper. Heat a couple of tablespoons of vegetable oil in a cast-iron skillet over medium-high heat. Add the lamb roast to the pan and brown it well on all sides. Transfer the browned roast to a covered roasting pan or oven-safe covered Dutch oven.

TOMATO BRAISING SAUCE

1. Preheat oven to 325°F. Mix all ingredients well and pour over the browned leg of lamb. Cover with a layer of aluminum foil before adding the lid. Place in the preheated oven to slowly braise for up to 3 hours.

2. Check on the roast about every hour, and if you feel the sauce is thickening too quickly, add a little more stock and turn the heat back to 300°F.

3. Remove the roast from the sauce and tent it under a sheet of aluminum foil to rest for 10-15 minutes before removing the strings and carving. Skim any excess fat off the tomato braising sauce and serve it with the lamb along with cooked orzo or other pasta.

One thing I've come to expect, while developing and posting new new food ideas on *Rock Recipes*, is the inevitable question that follows any really successful new main course that's posted: What do you serve with that? I think many people struggle with decisions on side dishes more than the foundation dish of the meal. It's a very relatable problem since the enjoyment of even the tenderest steak or perfectly roasted chicken can be improved with memorable side dishes that will have guests asking for the recipes. The side dishes here have proven to be consistent winners with our readers and are sure to be hits at your house too.

Soup is normally Spouse's specialty at our house. She's a real soup person. I swear she could have soup as a meal seven days a week. I'm more of a soup-as-appetizer person myself, but there are a couple of indulgent soups like my Lobster and Grilled Corn Chowder or good old fashioned Newfoundland Pea Soup and Dough Boys that are definitely fit for a meal in themselves.

Side Dishes *and* Soups

Creamy Parmesan and Bacon Potatoes

SERVES 4–6

6-8 slices of thick-sliced, good quality **smoked bacon**

2½ lbs of washed **potatoes**, skin on

¼ cup **garlic olive oil**

¼ cup **butter** (not margarine)

salt and **pepper** to season

1 cup **whipping cream**

¼ cup fresh grated **Parmesan cheese**

One of the hallmarks of a great steakhouse is not only the ability to produce a perfectly seasoned and cooked, juicy steak but incredible side dishes to go with it. I first had a version of these incredible potatoes at one such steakhouse. These are possibly the most indulgent potatoes I have ever eaten, combining crispy hash browns with crisp cooked bacon, all tossed in a creamy Parmesan sauce.

This is another of my "best guess" sort of recipes where I attempt to replicate something I've eaten at a restaurant. I've fried the potatoes here, but you could just as easily roast them tossed in a little garlic oil instead. Crisp cooked prosciutto could easily be substituted for the crisp bacon if you prefer.

tip > I make my own garlic oil by adding 1 cup of extra-virgin olive oil to a small saucepan on the lowest possible heat setting. Add 3-6 cloves of thinly sliced garlic to the pot, depending on how intensely flavoured you prefer the oil. Heat the oil for up to 15 minutes or so before removing it from the heat and allowing it to cool. You can remove the garlic slices immediately or leave them in to more intensely flavour the oil.

1. Cut in small pieces and crisp cook the bacon. Drain off all the fat and set the bacon aside.

2. Chop the washed potatoes into about ¾-inch dice.

3. Melt the garlic olive oil and butter together over medium heat in a large, heavy bottomed skillet. When heated, add the potatoes, season lightly with salt and pepper, and cook for about 20 minutes, turning the potatoes every few minutes. The potatoes should be fully cooked and crispy but not necessarily crispy on all sides. It's perfectly okay if they're a little "rustic." Remove the potatoes from the pan and keep warm in the oven as you prepare the sauce.

4. Reserve a few tablespoons of the oil and butter in the pan that the potatoes were cooked in. To this, add the whipping cream, and simmer until the cream is reduced by about half before melting in the grated Parmesan cheese.

5. Toss together the potatoes and bacon with the Parmesan cream sauce and serve.

Perfect Roast Potatoes

The straight-forward method of preparing these is also the secret to their success. The potatoes are parboiled before roasting, which loosens up the starches at the surface. A "dry" potato like the plain, dependable, old russet variety is best for roast potatoes because their surface starches break down more easily. The fat then combines with those surface starches to create a crispy exterior, which surrounds a piping hot, almost creamy center.

Fresh herbs and/or lemon zest can be added to the recipe to create different flavour versions. Less delicate herbs like rosemary and thyme work best, but add them only in the last 30 minutes or less of the cooking time so they don't burn.

SERVES 4–6

6 medium-sized **russet potatoes**, peeled

¼ cup **olive oil** (butter or other oil will work as well; a butter/olive oil combination is very good too)

½ tsp **kosher salt**

½ tsp **cracked black pepper**

1 whole **garlic bulb** broken into about 4 pieces (optional)

1. Parboil the potatoes in salted water for about 5 minutes. Some people prefer to boil them longer—up to 8 minutes or so. This will produce a thicker and crispier potato jacket if you prefer.

2. Meanwhile in a 375°F oven, heat a baking pan of sufficient size to hold your potatoes without crowding them. A glass or metal pan is fine as long as it's well heated beforehand. This will help to prevent the potatoes from sticking to the pan.

3. After parboiling, drain the potatoes and let them stand for 5 minutes. Then toss the potatoes with the olive oil, kosher salt, cracked black pepper, and garlic pieces.

4. Transfer the seasoned potatoes, garlic, and oil to the hot baking pan. These should sizzle as they hit the pan: a good indication that they won't stick. Roast the potatoes at 375°F for about 60-75 minutes or until they are nicely golden brown all over, turning them every 20 minutes or so. After the first 10 minutes, give the pan a shake to make sure the potatoes are not sticking. The roasted garlic may have to be removed before the potatoes are finished as it generally cooks faster.

Mediterranean Quinoa Salad

SERVES **6**

1 cup **quinoa**

½ tsp **salt**

1½ cups **water**

2 **tomatoes**, diced

1 cup diced **bell peppers**

1 cup diced **cucumber**

1 cup chopped **kalamata olives**

¼ cup chopped **green onion**

LEMON OREGANO DRESSING
¼ cup **extra-virgin olive oil**

2 tbsp **honey**

juice and finely minced **zest of 1 lemon**

2 tbsp chopped **fresh oregano** (or 1 tbsp dried oregano)

½ tsp **kosher salt**

½ tsp **black pepper**

We've been using quinoa at our house as a more nutritious substitute for rice and sometimes pasta, and the great thing about this recipe is that it can be served hot or cold. We serve it as a hot side dish with things like chicken souvlaki, and what's leftover gets served as a delicious cold quinoa salad the next day. For extra flavour, we sometimes add some crumbled feta cheese too.

1.   Over low heat, bring the quinoa, water, and salt to a boil. Cover and simmer slowly for 15-20 minutes until the grains are cooked but still a little firm to the bite. Remove from the heat, cover and let stand for 5-10 minutes. This additional siting time should allow any excess liquid to be absorbed.

2.   Remove the cover, fluff the quinoa with a fork, then add the tomatoes, bell peppers, cucumber, kalamata olives, and green onion.

3.   Toss everything together with the Lemon Oregano Dressing.

LEMON OREGANO DRESSING
1.   Whisk together well the virgin olive oil, honey, lemon juice and zest, oregano, kosher salt, and black pepper.

Bacon Cashew Brussels Sprouts

Brussels sprouts get a bad rap, but I think overcooking is generally what brings out the bitterness in these vegetables and makes them unpalatable to many folks. I just can't stand them when they're overcooked. As a general rule, if these sorts of vegetables lose their intense bright green colour and start to turn to dark green, then I refuse to eat them. It is a sure sign they've been overcooked to practically inedible.

I particularly like this recipe because I can pre-cook the Brussels sprouts ahead of time, immediately immerse them in ice water to stop the cooking action, and preserve their colour, then toss them in the garlic butter, bacon, and cashews to finish them off immediately before serving.

SERVES 6-8

2 lbs of **fresh Brussels sprouts,** trimmed and cut in half

8 slices **smoked bacon,** cut in small pieces

¼ cup **salted butter**

4 **cloves garlic,** minced

1 cup **toasted cashews**

juice of ½ **lemon**

1 tsp **cracked black pepper**

> tip > Quickly blanching many green vegetables like Brussels sprouts, green beans, and broccoli in rapidly boiling water for 2-3 minutes and then plunging them immediately into an ice water bath, locks in their bright green colour before freezing. Drain them from the ice water and spread in a single layer on parchment paper-lined cookie sheets to quick freeze them before storing in large Ziploc bags.

1. Boil the sprouts in salted water for 5 minutes before dropping them directly into a bowl of ice water to stop the cooking action.

2. In a large sauté pan, cook the smoked bacon until crisp. Drain all the bacon fat away and then add the butter and garlic. Cook only to soften the garlic. Don't brown it.

3. Toss the sprouts back into the pan with the garlic butter and bacon and add the cashews, lemon juice, and cracked black pepper. Toss together over high heat for only a minute or two until the sprouts are warmed through. Serve immediately.

Oven Baked Crispy Potato Wedge Fries

Think great crispy potato wedges have to be deep fried? Not on your life. At our house we never deep fry them. We parboil the potato wedges for only three minutes to break up the starches on the surface, which greatly aids in getting them fantastically crispy without a lot of oil. You can peel the potatoes if you prefer, but we like to keep the skins on for extra flavor and nutrition.

As the recipe notes, you can add herbs or chili flakes to the potatoes before baking, but you can also add flavour when they come out of the oven. Toss them in Cajun spice mix for a wonderful spicy version. As with roasting potatoes, we often break up a head of garlic and simply throw the unpeeled cloves randomly among the wedges to infuse garlic flavor into the oil and potatoes.

SERVES 4–6

6 large **potatoes** (about 1½-2 lbs)

3 tbsp **olive oil** or **canola oil**

salt and **pepper** to season

1. Preheat the oven to 425°F. Preheat the cookie sheet in the oven as well. It's important that the fries hit a hot pan because this will help ensure they don't stick. If the potato wedges sizzle when they hit the hot pan, that's perfect. You'll want to get the pan back into the oven as quickly as possible too.

2. Bring 2-3 liters of salted water to a boil. Begin by washing the potatoes and cutting them in thick wedges. Drop the potato wedges in the boiling water and cook for 3 minutes exactly. Immediately drain the water off the potatoes and toss in the olive oil, salt, and pepper. You can add additional seasoning at this point, like herbs or chili flakes, but these potatoes are great simply seasoned with salt and pepper.

3. Spread the potato wedges in a single layer on a large preheated cookie sheet. Bake in the preheated oven for about 30 minutes. Turn the wedges over halfway through the baking time. Remove from oven, sprinkle with kosher salt, and serve.

Sweet Mustard and Bacon Potato Salad

SERVES 6–8

3 lbs washed, unpeeled **red potatoes**, diced large

½ cup jarred, mayonnaise type, **salad dressing**

¼ cup **plain yellow mustard**

2 tbsp **apple cider vinegar**

3 tbsp **white sugar**

1 small **red bell pepper**, diced small

2 tbsp minced **red onion**

3 tbsp chopped **capers**

3 tbsp chopped **cilantro** (or parsley)

8 slices **smoked bacon**, cooked crisp and roughly chopped

½ tsp **freshly ground black pepper**

pinch of **salt**

This recipe was inspired by a couple of different potato salads that I combined into one and then borrowed the dressing, a sweet mustard sauce, from a third recipe we often served with cold cuts and potato salad as a kid. It makes a great take-along item to potlucks and a superb addition to summer picnics, cookouts, or barbeques. As one *Rock Recipes* reader noted, "You can't have too many potato salad recipes!"

1. Simmer the diced potatoes slowly in boiling salted water just until fork tender. Do not overcook the potatoes or they will fall apart in the salad.

2. Drain the potatoes and scatter them on a cookie sheet to cool quickly. I usually put the cookie sheet in the fridge for 30 minutes or so to cool off completely.

3. Mix together the salad dressing, plain yellow mustard, apple cider vinegar, sugar, red pepper, red onion, capers, cilantro, bacon, black pepper, and a pinch of salt.

4. Pour the dressing over the cold potatoes and toss well. Store in an airtight container in the fridge until ready to serve.

EASY CAESAR SALAD DRESSING

2 **cloves garlic**, finely minced

½ tsp **anchovy paste** (optional)

½ cup **plain mayonnaise**

juice of ½ **lemon**

zest of ½ lemon, finely minced (optional)

1 oz **white wine vinegar**

2 tbsp fresh chopped **Italian parsley**

½ tsp **Dijon mustard**

¼ cup freshly grated **Parmesan cheese**

½ tsp **freshly ground black pepper**

sea salt to taste

2 tbsp **extra-virgin olive oil**

RADICCHIO ALMOND CAESAR SALAD

1 large head **romaine lettuce**, chopped, washed, and dried

1 small **red onion**, very thinly sliced

½ cup **golden raisins**

¼ cup **toasted slivered almonds**

¼ cup freshly grated **Parmesan cheese**

6 slices sugar-cured **smoked bacon**, crisp fried and chopped

1 small head **radicchio**, chopped, washed, and dried

½ cup **Easy Caesar Salad Dressing**

Radicchio Almond Caesar Salad

Many chefs claim that a perfect dish combines sweet, salty, bitter, and sour tastes. Perhaps this is why I love this salad so much. The sweetness of the golden raisins, the smoky saltiness of the bacon, the slightly bitter edge of the radicchio, and the pungent, slightly sour note of good Parmesan cheese all combine to make what may be the perfect salad. Add to that sweet red onion and the nutty flavor of toasted almonds and you'll probably omit the "may" portion of that last sentence. Highly recommended!

EASY CAESAR SALAD DRESSING

1. Combine all ingredients in a blender or food processor until well blended.

RADICCHIO ALMOND CAESAR SALAD

1. Toss all the ingredients and the Easy Caesar Salad Dressing very well together just before serving.

Gruyere and Thyme Potatoes Dauphinoise

SERVES 6-8

2 lbs **Yukon gold** (yellow) **potatoes**

2 cups **heavy cream** (whipping cream)

1 cup **milk**

1 **shallot**, finely diced

1 tbsp **fresh thyme leaves**

½ tsp freshly grated **nutmeg**

¾ tsp **salt**

½ tsp **ground black pepper**

2 cups grated **Gruyere cheese** (1 cup for each of the two layers)

Potatoes Dauphinoise is just a posh name for scalloped potatoes, but the cooking method may also differ from your favourite scalloped potato recipe. This is a great basic recipe that our family loves, and it's very adaptable as well. Switch up the cheese and/or herbs and change the spices and seasoning to create your own favourite version. I find yellow or red or other varieties of waxy potatoes work best here and hold up well in a hot oven. Drier, fluffier potato varieties like russets tend to break down too much and get mushy during the cooking process.

> **tip** > With any scalloped potato recipe, it's beneficial to boil the potato slices for several minutes, either in a cream mixture, if you're using one, or just plain salted water if you're using a white sauce. Those few minutes of preparation will cut down considerably on the oven time for the recipe.

1. Peel and thinly slice the potatoes. Bring them to a slow simmer in a large saucepan or Dutch oven, along with the heavy cream, milk, diced shallot, thyme leaves, grated nutmeg, salt, and ground black pepper. Simmer for 10 minutes.

2. Preheat oven to 350°F. Drain the potatoes from the pot, reserving the cream mixture. Layer the potatoes in a shallow baking pan in two layers, adding the Gruyere cheese between the layers.

3. Pour the reserved cream mixture over the potatoes and bake in the preheated oven for about 1 hour until the top is golden brown and the potatoes are fork tender.

4 cups diced **white onions**

6 **cloves garlic**

1 cup **water**

3 tbsp **olive oil** (you can use clarified butter or ghee if you prefer)

2 cups **canned crushed tomatoes**

2 tbsp freshly grated **ginger root**

½ cup **ground toasted almonds**

1 cup **coconut milk**

½ small **red chili**, minced (more or less to taste)

2 tsp **turmeric**

1 tsp **cinnamon**

½ tsp **ground cardamom**

4 tsp mild **yellow curry powder**

½ tsp **nutmeg**

1 tsp **salt**

1 tsp **black pepper**

1 tsp **ground coriander seed**

2 tsp **garam masala**

½ tsp **ground cloves**

pinch of **saffron** (optional)

½ tsp **cumin**

1 tbsp **brown sugar**

4 cups **canned chick peas**, rinsed

1 cup **plain low-fat yogurt**

Coconut Chick Pea Korma

This is one of my son's favourite dishes. He loves his Indian food and thinks this makes a great side dish for an Indian meal, like our delicious Butter Chicken, or as a satisfying lunch all on its own with some naan flatbread. We also serve this side with grilled chicken or pork chops simply seasoned with salt, pepper, and garam masala or curry powder. Make a big batch because this is one of those things that's even better as reheated leftovers.

---

1. For the sauce, begin by pureeing together the diced white onions, 6 cloves of garlic, and 1 cup water.

2. In a large saucepan heat the olive oil. Add the pureed onion mixture and cook over medium heat for a few minutes, stirring constantly. Then add the crushed tomatoes, ginger root, toasted almonds, coconut milk, minced red chili, turmeric, cinnamon, cardamom, curry powder, nutmeg, salt, pepper, coriander seed, garam masala, ground cloves, saffron, cumin, and brown sugar.

3. Simmer slowly for about 20 minutes then add the chick peas and low-fat yogurt. Simmer for an additional 15 minutes. Serve with steamed jasmine rice and/or naan.

Maple Roasted Vegetables

2 **carrots**, thickly sliced

2 **parsnips**, thickly sliced

1 large **red onion**, cut in wedges

1 **lemon**, cut in half or quarters

1 small **butternut squash**, cut in chunks

4 **cloves garlic**, unpeeled

6 **yellow beets**, quartered

4 tbsp **olive oil**

pinch of **salt**

pinch of **black pepper**

2-3 tbsp **pure maple syrup**

We adore our roast potatoes here in the Parsons household, but truth be told, whenever they're in the oven, they're most likely sharing space with other roasted vegetables, especially carrots and parsnips. A visit to our local farmers market, especially during autumn harvest, often results in a beautiful collection of vegetables to roast with our Sunday dinner. I only add the maple syrup to these vegetables after they're partially cooked, so the sugar in the syrup doesn't burn. This allows the veggies to caramelize a little before the light glaze of maple syrup finishes them off.

1. Preheat the oven to 350°F. Toss all of the ingredients, except the maple syrup, together with the olive oil.

2. Roast in a single layer in a large baking dish (about 9x13 inches) in the preheated oven for approximately 30 minutes or until all of the vegetables are fork tender. Toss the vegetables once during the 30 minutes.

3. Squeeze the roasted lemon pieces over the rest of the vegetables and add the maple syrup. Toss together well to coat all the vegetables, and roast for about another 30 minutes or until all of the vegetables are fork tender.

4. Toss the vegetables several times during the last of the cooking time to glaze the vegetables in the maple syrup.

Apple Pecan Cornbread Stuffing

SERVES 8–10

CORNBREAD

1 cup **yellow cornmeal**

¾ cup + 2 tbsp **all-purpose flour**

2 tbsp **sugar**

1½ tsp **baking powder**

¼ tsp **baking soda**

2 large **eggs**

1½ cups **buttermilk** (or milk soured with 1-2 tbsp lemon juice)

APPLE PECAN CORNBREAD STUFFING

2 tbsp **olive oil**

3 **cloves garlic**, minced

1 large **onion**, diced small

1 stalk **celery**, diced small (optional)

4-5 cups large **cornbread cubes**

2 **apples**, diced

2 tbsp chopped **fresh thyme** (or oregano)

½ tsp **freshly ground black pepper**

pinch of **salt**

¼ cup melted **butter**

1 **egg**

1 cup **chicken** or **vegetable stock**

¾ cup **pecans**

Cornbread stuffing is not something I make often because there's rarely enough leftover cornbread to make it. Since cornbread really takes just a few minutes to throw together, it's really worth the effort to whip up a quick batch to enjoy this apple and pecan stuffing. It's the perfect accompaniment to a juicy and delicious glazed pork loin but would be equally as good served with roast chicken or turkey or even with a baked ham dinner.

CORNBREAD

1. Preheat oven to 350°F. To prepare the cornbread, sift together the cornmeal, flour, sugar, baking powder, and baking soda. Add the eggs and milk and beat together until smooth.

2. Pour batter into a well-greased 9x9-inch baking dish and bake in the preheated oven for about 30 minutes or until a wooden toothpick inserted in the center comes out clean. Cool completely before using in the stuffing.

APPLE PECAN CORNBREAD STUFFING

1. Preheat oven to 350°F. Grease an 8x8-inch baking dish well with butter.

2. Heat the olive oil in a sauté pan and add the garlic, onions, and celery. Cook just until the onions have softened but not browned. Toss the cooked onion mixture with the cornbread cubes, apples, thyme, salt, pepper, and melted butter.

3. Place the cornbread mixture evenly into the greased baking dish. Whisk together the eggs and chicken or vegetable stock well and pour evenly over the cornbread mixture. Sprinkle the pecans over the top. Bake for 30-35 minutes or until the center is set.

Curried Fried Basmati Rice
with Red Lentils

This mildly spiced side dish is one to plan when you're serving rice and/or lentils with another meal during the week. Cook more than you need to serve on the first day and just store the rest in the fridge to make an easy addition to another dinner, even days later.

While it goes wonderfully well when serving Indian inspired dishes like my Quick and Easy Butter Chicken (recipe on page 24), this aromatic side dish makes a welcome, flavourful addition to meals that include simple grilled chicken, pork, lamb, or even grilled fish.

SERVES 4–6

4 tbsp **canola oil**

2 **cloves garlic**, minced

1½ tbsp **yellow curry powder**

1 tsp **garam masala**

1 tbsp freshly grated **ginger root**

salt and **pepper** to season

3 cups cooked **basmati rice**

¾ cup firm cooked **red lentils**

3-4 tbsp chopped **fresh, cilantro, coriander** or **chives** (or a combination)

1. In a wok or large sauté pan over medium-high heat, heat the oil, garlic, curry powder, and garam masala. Cook together for just a minute to slightly soften the garlic and release the flavour of the spices.

2. Add the ginger and sauté for another few seconds before adding the cooked rice and lentils.

3. Season with salt and pepper and toss together continuously until the rice and lentils are thoroughly heated.

4. Finish by tossing in the herbs for the last minute of cooking time and serve immediately.

Newfoundland Style
Ham and Split Pea Soup *with* Dough Boys

NEWFOUNDLAND STYLE HAM AND SPLIT PEA SOUP

12 **cups water**

1 **ham bone**

4 **cloves garlic**, roughly chopped

1 large **carrot**, coarsely grated

1 small **onion**, chopped

2 cups **dried yellow split peas**

3-4 **bay leaves**

1 tbsp **dried thyme**

1 tsp **coarsely ground white** or **black pepper**, your preference

1 large **red** or **sweet white onion**, about 1½ cups diced (yellow onions are traditional, but I use sweeter onions to balance the saltiness of the ham.)

3 cups diced **carrots**

3 cups diced **baked smoked ham**

option > You can replace the ham in this recipe with traditional salt beef (see the note at the end of the recipe directions)

DOUGH BOYS (MAKES ABOUT 10)

2 cups **flour**

2 tbsp **sugar**

1 tsp **baking soda**

2 tsp **baking powder**

½ tsp **salt**

1 cup **warm milk**

¼ cup melted **butter**

Everyone—and I mean everyone—who's grown up in Newfoundland has had pea soup and dough boys. "Dough boys" is the local name for what folks in most parts of North America would refer to as dumplings: very simple, flour-based dough balls dropped into simmering soups or stews to gently cook to fluffy perfection in the last few minutes before the meal is served.

This is a terrific meal idea for a time-pressed workday. Since popular wisdom suggests pea soup is always better the next day, why not make a big pot on the weekend and warm it up the next day. The dough boys can be ready in about 15 minutes, so there's one quick and delicious weekday dinner sorted.

Like all soups at our house, we freeze this in individual servings for quick lunches too.

NEWFOUNDLAND STYLE HAM AND SPLIT PEA SOUP

1. Fill a large pot with 12 cups of water. Add the ham bone, garlic, carrot, and onion. Cover and simmer slowly for 1½ hours. Strain the stock through a colander and return it to the pot. Skim excess fat from the surface of the stock.

2. Add split peas, bay leaves, thyme, pepper, and onion (if using salt beef, add it here).

3. I don't add any salt at this point. The salt content of the ham will determine if you need to add a little at the end. Let your own taste be the guide. Simmer slowly and gently for about 45 minutes, stirring occasionally so the peas do not stick to the bottom of the pot. Then add the diced carrots and diced baked smoked ham.

4. Simmer for an additional 10 minutes, stirring occasionally. Taste the soup at this point to determine if any additional salt is necessary. In all likelihood, it will not. Now add the dough boys to a very gently simmering pot.

DOUGH BOYS

1. Sift together the flour, sugar, baking soda, baking powder, and salt. With a wooden spoon, very quickly mix in the warm milk and melted butter.

2. Do *not* over-work this dough. Stir in the liquid as quickly as possible, and as soon as a soft dough forms, *stop* mixing. Make sure you give the soup one last good stir to make sure nothing sticks to the bottom of the pot then immediately drop the dough by heaping tablespoonfuls into the slowly simmering soup. Put the cover on the pot and do *not* remove it for 15 minutes. After 15 minutes, remove the dough boys from the pot, give the soup a final stir, and remove the bay leaves before serving.

note > Traditional Newfoundland pea soup would have been very simply seasoned with only yellow onions, pepper, and salt if necessary. Garlic, thyme, and bay leaves would have been unknown in these parts to my grandmother's generation, so if you want to enjoy the traditional version, please feel free to omit these ingredients. I believe all food cultures are continuously evolving, so I tend to meld the old with the new to create my updated versions of many recipes. Occasionally though, it's always good to pay homage to our culinary heritage by preparing the simple and delicious version that so many have enjoyed and gained sustenance from for generations.

In Newfoundland, salt brined, cured beef is also a very traditional ingredient in split pea soup. You can replace the ham in this recipe with about half the amount of salt beef. Just be sure to soak the salt beef in water for 24 hours before using it in the soup, and please change the water at least once during that time, or you risk your soup being far too salty. Cut the salt beef in small cubes and add to the pot with the peas and use water or vegetable stock instead of ham stock. (Corned beef is also a good choice if salt beef is not available in your area.)

Turkey and Black Bean Soup

Spouse loves her soups, and she's always whipping up another quick-and-easy, wholesome soup like this one using leftover turkey. A few quality ingredients and a very simple preparation is all it takes to enjoy this healthy meal option. This is a soup we often freeze in individual portions in sealed plastic containers to provide a quick workday lunch any day of the week.

2 medium **carrots**, coarsely grated

1 medium **red onion**, diced small

3 **cloves garlic**, minced

6 cups of **turkey** or **chicken stock**

one 28 oz can of **tomatoes**

one 19 oz can of **black beans**, rinsed and drained

2 cups of chopped, cooked **turkey**

3 tbsp **fresh oregano**

salt and **pepper** to taste

1. In a large pot, cook the grated carrots, diced red onion, and garlic until soft. Then add the turkey or chicken stock, tomatoes, black beans, cooked turkey, oregano, salt, and pepper. Simmer over medium heat for 20 minutes.

Lobster and Grilled Corn Chowder
with Grilled Lemon

SERVES 4–6

1½-2 lb **lobster**, cooked, de-shelled, and diced

2 **cloves garlic**, minced

1 large **white onion**, chopped

2 tbsp **butter**

2 tbsp **olive oil**

2 stalks **celery**, diced small

pinch of **salt**

½ tsp **white pepper**

3-4 tbsp **flour**

4 cups **1% partly skimmed milk**, scalded

2-3 cups **low-sodium seafood stock** (or low-sodium chicken stock)

3 tbsp chopped **fresh chives**

2 tbsp chopped **fresh thyme leaves**

salt and **pepper** to season

5-6 ears **grilled sweet corn** (just turn it on a hot grill until the surface begins to char then cut it off the cob with a sharp knife.)

charred lemon wedges

Here's a great New England style chowder that combines two great central ingredients: grilled sweet corn and succulent lobster. The sweetness of the grilled corn pairs well with the rich lobster meat without being too overpowering. The pop of the sweet corn adds a delicious textural difference as well.

This chowder makes a spectacular first course at a dinner party, or serve it with some garlic toast and a small side salad as a luxurious lunch. We recently served cups of this chowder to guests at a weekend barbeque and it was very well received by all who sampled it. The quickly grilled lemon wedges get served with the chowder to be squeezed in before eating for a final layer of flavour and burst of freshness.

> **tip** > You can make your own seafood stock by slowly simmering shrimp, crab, or lobster shells and any fish trimmings with chopped garlic, onions, and celery, then straining. I collect shrimp shells, small lobster legs, and fish trimmings from other meals in the freezer until I have enough to make a small pot of stock. Remember that the slower you simmer any stock, the clearer its final appearance will be.

1. You can buy your lobster pre-steamed if you like, but I like to cook it myself by under cooking about 5 minutes and then finishing off the lobster by simmering it in the soup. If you're using pre-cooked lobster, add it as close to the end of the cooking time as possible so it doesn't overcook and become rubbery.

2. Sauté the garlic, onion, butter, olive oil, celery, salt, and white pepper in a medium-sized pot over medium heat until the onions begin to soften but not brown. Then add the flour.

3. Cook for a couple of minutes over medium heat, stirring constantly. The flour should foam a little but not brown. Quickly stir in the scalded part-skimmed milk, seafood stock, chives, thyme, salt and pepper, and grilled sweet corn.

4. Simmer slowly for 10-15 minutes, stirring occasionally. In the last few minutes of cooking time, add the lobster. Serve immediately with lemon wedges that have been charred on a hot grill or in a cast-iron grill pan.

Roasted Tomato and Fennel Soup

SERVES 6

8 large **ripe tomatoes**, diced

1 large **fennel bulb**, diced
about ½ inch

1 medium **red onion**, diced

4 **cloves garlic**, chopped

4 tbsp **olive oil**

2 tbsp **brown sugar**

½ tsp **crushed chillies** (optional,
or to taste)

3 tbsp **balsamic vinegar**

salt and **pepper** to season

8 cups **vegetable stock** (salt free
or low sodium are best)

2 tbsp chopped **fresh thyme**

2 tbsp **smoked paprika**

This is such a simple soup but oh so flavorful with oven-roasted tomato, fennel with a little earthy thyme, fragrant smoked paprika, and a touch of spice. This would make an ideal starter course or a fantastic lunch with a great grilled-cheese sandwich. We freeze this soup in individual portions too as a terrific alternative to having to use a can opener for a quick meal any time.

1. Preheat oven to 350°F. Toss the diced tomatoes, fennel, red onion, chopped garlic, olive oil, brown sugar, crushed chillies, balsamic vinegar, salt, and pepper in a shallow baking dish and bake in the preheated oven. Cook for about 60-70 minutes, stirring occasionally or until the fennel pieces are very soft, most of the liquid has cooked off, and the tomato and fennel reach a good chunky consistency.

2. Once cooked, puree the mixture well in a blender or food processor and pour into a soup pot. Then add vegetable stock, thyme, and smoked paprika to the pot.

3. Simmer for 20-30 minutes or until the soup reaches your desired consistency. Taste and do a final seasoning of salt and pepper if necessary.

Lemon Chicken and Red Quinoa Soup

This recipe was created after a delicious lemon chicken dinner using the stock made from the carcass of the bird. Of course, you don't need to have enjoyed that great roast chicken dinner to enjoy this soup. Simply take about 3 boneless, skinless chicken breasts and marinate them in lemon juice and your choice of fresh or dried herbs for a half-hour, then grill or broil them until fully cooked. If using store-bought chicken stock, make sure you choose no sodium or low sodium. It's always better to season the soup yourself to control the amount of salt.

When serving this soup, you can sprinkle on some fresh herbs at the end and serve with a wedge of lemon to be squeezed into the bowl just before serving to add a little extra brightness to the soup.

SERVES 4–6

1 medium **onion**

3 **cloves garlic**, chopped

1 cup diced **carrots**

1 cup diced **celery**, include the leaves as well

6 cups **chicken stock**

2 diced **tomatoes**

½ cup **red quinoa**

½ tsp **black pepper**

1 tsp **dry thyme**

½ tsp **salt** (or to taste)

½ cup **corn kernels**

2 cups cooked and diced **lemon chicken**

1. In a large pot, sauté together the onions, garlic, diced carrots, and diced celery until the onions have softened. Then add the chicken stock, diced tomatoes, red quinoa, black pepper, thyme, and salt.

2. Simmer for about 30 minutes or until the quinoa and carrots are fully cooked. In the last few minutes of cooking time, add the corn and diced lemon chicken.

3. Serve with added chopped fresh herbs and a lemon wedge to squeeze into the individual bowls.

Scallop and Lemongrass Soup

SERVES 4

4 cups of good quality, low-sodium **vegetable broth**

1 tsp **black peppercorns**

½ **red chilli**, diced

sea salt to season

1 large piece of **lemon grass**, chopped in 3-inch lengths and crushed with a mallet or the back of a knife

3 tbsp roughly chopped **cilantro** (I like tarragon or dill as substitutes too)

½ lb small **scallops**, about the size of the top of your thumb

4 **lime wedges**

finely diced **red bell pepper** (or diced chilli if you like it hotter)

We try to keep our food pretty simple and easy at our house, even when throwing a dinner party. This simple soup is an example of how to take a relaxed approach to food and still present a dish that, with very few ingredients, is still quite elegant. Nothing could be simpler than this appetizer soup that never fails to get a few *oohs* and *ahs* when it arrives at the table.

This soup really is just small scallops poached in a flavourful broth, but the recipe's a great example of how using quality, fresh ingredients can make all the difference in creating something uncomplicated and completely delicious.

> tip > You can always use homemade vegetable stock, but if choosing store-bought stock, select salt free or low sodium. This gives you the ability to better control the seasoning in your broth. Remember that when simmering and reducing store-bought stock for soups and sauces, you are concentrating the amount of salt contained in it, so it's better to start with a stock that contains a minimum of salt.

1. To make the broth, combine the vegetable broth, black peppercorns, red chilli, sea salt, lemon grass, and chopped cilantro in a large pot.

2. Bring the broth to a boil first, then turn down the heat and add the peppercorns, chilli, salt, lemongrass, and cilantro. This broth is more steeped than boiled. Try to keep the pot at a very slow simmer or just at the edge of boiling. This helps keep the broth more clear too.

3. Steep the broth for about 20 minutes or so before straining it through a fine sieve and discarding everything but the liquid. Just before serving, bring the broth back up to a slow boil then add the scallops. Now when the broth begins to simmer again, remove the pan from the heat immediately. Cover and let it sit for 5 minutes to poach the scallops.

4. To serve the soup, strain the scallops off the broth and divide them evenly between four bowls, stacking them at the center of the bowl.

5. Squeeze a wedge of lime over each of the bowls of scallops. Then ladle the broth gently into the bowl and garnish with diced red pepper and a sprinkle of chopped cilantro.

Weekends are often the best opportunity to experiment in the kitchen for many working folks, and while an invitation to my house on the weekend usually means a sit-down Sunday roast or slow-cooked dinner, in recent years I've come to really love a great weekend brunch. If I'm entertaining friends or family nowadays, they might just as likely be invited to a late morning meal ranging from simple breakfast fare to truly indulgent offerings like Crab Cakes Eggs Benedict.

Most people love to go to a good restaurant for brunch, so why not create something special and invite them over? Homemade touches are key to a great brunch. Everyone appreciates fantastic baked goodies like fluffy buttermilk biscuits with honey butter or decadent flavour combinations baked into light, delicious scones. Preparing homemade sausage patties can be as easy as mixing ground pork with a great blend of herbs and spices. It's the little efforts that are sure to impress your guests and make the late morning feel like a special occasion.

Brunch

The Best Buttermilk Biscuits
with Honey Butter

MAKES ABOUT 18 TWO-INCH BISCUITS

BEST BUTTERMILK BISCUITS

4 cups all-purpose flour

9 tsp baking powder
(this amount gives plenty of quick lift, but you can reduce it a little if you prefer)

½ tsp baking soda

¼ cup + 1 tbsp very cold vegetable shortening, cut in small cubes

¼ cup + 1 tbsp very cold salted butter, cut in small cubes

2 cups buttermilk

HONEY BUTTER

1 cup butter

½ cup honey

There are a few tips that make this recipe work particularly well in my opinion. While many traditional southern recipes call for all shortening in varying amounts, some of which leave the biscuits a little too oily for my taste, this one relies on a combination of vegetable shortening and butter for a perfect combination of lightness and flavour.

The trick to really flaky biscuits is handling the dough as little as possible. Overworking the dough will produce much denser biscuits. I like to fold the dough about 3 or 4 times when rolling it out to create flaky layers, but the key is to work quickly as you do so. A higher than usual oven temperature also makes these rise, bake, and brown quickly, making them extra flaky too. Once you've cut your biscuits out and placed them on the baking sheet, I find that letting them rest for 5 minutes at room temperature can also help make them a little lighter.

Large biscuits make great breakfast sandwiches too, especially with my Easy Homemade Breakfast Sausage (see page 188).

BEST BUTTERMILK BISCUITS

1. Preheat oven to 425°F. In a food processor, blend together all-purpose flour, baking powder, and baking soda. Pulse in the cold vegetable shortening (I store mine in the freezer) and the cold salted butter. Do not over incorporate the shortening and butter into the flour. Similar to making a flaky pastry, small pieces of butter should be visible in the flour. You can use a pastry cutter or two knives placed between your fingers to cut in the shortening and butter if you don't have a food processor.

2. Transfer this mixture from the food processor into a large mixing bowl and make a well in the center. Pour in the buttermilk.

3. Working very quickly with a wooden spoon, fold the dry mixture through the buttermilk, only until the flour disappears, then stop immediately. Drop the sticky dough onto a well-floured countertop or bread board. Sprinkle the top of the dough with additional flour as well as flouring your hands to handle the dough. Roll out the dough, folding it 3 or 4 times before rolling out to a final thickness of about 1 to 1½ inches. Using a sharp 2-inch biscuit cutter, cut the biscuits out and place them, almost touching, on a parchment paper-lined baking sheet. I recommend aluminum baking sheets because they tolerate the higher oven temperature without burning the bottom of the biscuits.

4. Bake in the preheated oven for about 20 minutes or until the tops of the biscuits are evenly golden brown. Delicious served warm with Honey Butter.

HONEY BUTTER

1. Honey butter is simply honey beaten into plain butter in a 2 to 1 ratio of butter to honey. Combine the butter (not margarine) and honey. Beat together with an electric mixer until smooth and fluffy.

Raspberry White Chocolate Scones

MAKES **8** LARGE SCONES OR
ABOUT **18** SMALLER SCONES

3 cups flour

½ cup sugar

6 tsp baking powder

½ tsp salt

¾ cup very cold butter, cubed

6 oz good quality chopped white chocolate

2 tbsp lemon juice

2 tsp vanilla extract

1 cup milk

1½ cups frozen raspberries

tip > I start these in my food processor because it's so fast, but they can be made just as easily in a large bowl by cutting the butter in with a pastry blender or even 2 knives held between the fingers.

My sister, Belinda, texted once from the ski slopes in Jasper, Alberta, to rave about a white chocolate and raspberry scone she'd found there. It sounded pretty darn good to me, and as regular readers of *Rock Recipes* know, I'm very fond of all things scone related, so how could I not try to invent a version of my own.

1. In a food processor, combine the flour, sugar, baking powder, and salt. Cut in the very cold, cubed butter, and pulse process until this mixture resembles a coarse meal. It's very important that pea-sized pieces of butter remain in the mixture. Remove to a large bowl and toss in the chopped white chocolate.

2. Mix together the lemon juice, vanilla extract, and milk. Pour this over the surface of the dry mixture. Toss all together gently with a fork only enough to form a dough ball. When the flour is almost incorporated, add the frozen raspberries. Frozen berries work best because they're less delicate and easier to incorporate into the scone dough.

3. Work this dough as little as possible or the finished scones will be too dense and heavy. Roll to 1-inch thickness and cut out scones with a biscuit cutter or in triangles with a sharp knife and place on a parchment-lined baking sheet.

4. If desired, you can brush the tops of the scones with an egg wash of 1 egg beaten together with 1 tbsp water. You can sprinkle the tops with turbinado sugar if desired, but this is, of course, optional.

5. Bake at 375°F for 25 minutes or until light golden brown. Baking time will vary depending on the size of your biscuit cutter.

Blueberry Cheesecake Scones

Man, are these ever scrumptious! Warm, tender scones with crispy, sugary edges, bursting with juicy blueberries and with chunks of vanilla cheesecake baked right in. If you bake at all or ever wanted to start, you simply must try these outstanding scones. Then invite someone over, sit back, and collect the compliments.

MAKES 12 LARGE SCONES

**CHEESECAKE
(PREPARED THE PREVIOUS DAY)**

one 8 oz block cream cheese

⅓ cup sugar

2 tsp vanilla extract

1 egg

SCONES

3 cups flour

½ cup sugar

6 tsp baking powder

½ tsp salt

¾ cup very cold butter, cubed

6 oz good quality chopped white chocolate

2 tbsp lemon juice

2 tsp vanilla extract

1 cup milk (add a little more if necessary)

1½ cups blueberries

frozen cheesecake cubes

NOTE: You will need to prepare the cheesecake the previous day so you can freeze it overnight.

1.   To prepare the cheesecake, mix together the cream cheese, sugar, vanilla extract, and egg. Pour into a parchment-lined loaf pan. (Small silicone loaf pans are perfect for this purpose.)

2.   Bake at 300°F for about 25-30 minutes or until the center of the cheesecake is set. Cool completely before placing in the freezer overnight. Remove the parchment paper from the cheesecake and cut it into ½-inch cubes. Return the frozen cubes to the freezer until ready to add to the scone dough.

3.   I start the scone dough in my food processor because it's so fast, but they can be made just as easily in a large bowl by cutting the butter in with a pastry blender or even 2 knifes held between the fingers.

4.   In a food processor, combine flour, sugar, baking powder, and salt. Cut in the very cold, cubed butter. Pulse process until this mixture resembles a coarse meal. Pea-sized pieces of butter should remain in this mixture. Remove to a large bowl and toss in the chopped white chocolate.

5.   In a separate bowl, mix together the lemon juice, vanilla extract, and milk, and pour this over the surface of the dry mixture. Toss all together gently with a fork only enough to form a dough ball. When the flour is almost incorporated, fold in the blueberries and the frozen cheesecake cubes prepared the day before.

6. Frozen berries work well too because they're less delicate and easier to incorporate into the scone dough. It's important that you work this dough as little as possible, or the finished scones will be too dense and heavy. Roll to 1-inch thickness and cut out scones with a biscuit cutter or in triangles with a sharp knife and place on a parchment-lined baking sheet.

7. If desired, you can brush the tops of the scones with an egg wash of 1 egg beaten together with 1 tbsp water. You can sprinkle the tops with turbinado sugar if desired, but this is, of course, optional.

8. Bake at 375°F for 25 minutes or until light golden brown. Baking time will vary depending on the size of your biscuit cutter.

Rum Raisin Cinnamon Roll Sticky Buns

MAKES 1 DOZEN LARGE ROLLS

3 cups all-purpose flour

¼ cup sugar

1 pkg (5 g) instant dry yeast

¼ tsp salt

½ cup + 3 tbsp melted butter

1¼ cups warm milk

2 eggs, slightly beaten

2 tsp vanilla extract

2 cups brown sugar (in two, 1 cup portions)

3 oz dark rum

½ cup very soft butter

2 tsp cinnamon

1-1½ cups golden raisins

Now wouldn't the sight of these at a weekend brunch make your heart skip a beat? This has to be the most delicious sticky bun I have ever eaten, and Spouse says ditto for her. Rum and raisin is her favourite ice-cream flavour, so I had her in mind when I decided to create a whole new version of this brunch standout.

1. Combine 2 cups of the flour along with the sugar, instant yeast, and salt in a large bowl or in the bowl of a large electric mixer that uses a dough hook. Add 3 tbsp of melted butter, the warm milk, eggs, and vanilla extract.

2. Using a wooden spoon or the regular paddle of your electric mixer, beat for 4-5 minutes until the mixture is smooth with no lumps. If using an electric mixer, switch to the dough hook at this point and begin to slowly incorporate the remaining 1 cup of flour. If not using an electric mixer, keep mixing in the flour gradually until a soft dough forms that leaves the sides of the bowl. You may need to use a little less or a little more flour. This is not uncommon.

3. Knead the dough for an additional 10 minutes either in the electric mixer or on a bread board or countertop. Cover the dough and leave to rest and rise for 30-60 minutes. While the dough is rising, make the rum and butter caramel by bringing to a boil, over medium heat, 1 cup of the brown sugar and ½ cup of melted butter. Whisk the butter and brown sugar together to ensure they're well incorporated. When the mixture begins to foam nicely, remove from the heat and quickly whisk in the dark rum.

4. Be very careful when whisking in the rum. The sugar mixture will be very hot, and the rum will likely begin to immediately steam up and boil, but this all calms down quite quickly. The alcohol may flame briefly, so make sure you add it at arm's length. Just wait for the flame to subside before pouring the caramel into the bottom of a well-greased 9x13-inch baking pan.

5. Punch the dough down and knead it for a few minutes by hand before letting it rest for another 10 minutes. Roll the rested dough out into a large rectangle about 12x18 inches.

6. Combine the ½ cup of very soft butter, the other 1cup of brown sugar, and the cinnamon. Spread this mixture over the rolled-out dough and sprinkle on the raisins.

7. Starting at the short side of the rectangle, roll the dough into a log, pinching the dough together to seal at the end of the roll. Cut the roll into 12 equal pieces and place in the bottom of a greased 9x13-inch baking pan on top of the caramel sauce.

8. Cover the baking pan with a clean tea towel and allow the rolls to rise until at least doubled in size, about 1½-2 hours. (I sometimes let them rise in the fridge overnight and pop them into the oven in the morning. I've also frozen them before they rise and take them out of the freezer to rise overnight on the countertop before going to bed. If they have not doubled in size by morning, leave them in a warm kitchen for about 30 minutes to finish rising.)

9. Bake at 350°F for 40-45 minutes or until the rolls spring back when touched in the middle of the pan. Let rest in the pan for a few minutes before inverting the rolls onto a large serving platter or bread board.

Cherry Swirl Almond Crumble Coffee Cake

SERVES 12

CHERRY COMPOTE

2 cups pitted cherries

½ cup sugar

1 oz + 3 tbsp water

1 rounded tbsp cornstarch

COFFEE CAKE

2⅔ cups flour

3 tsp baking powder

2 eggs

1¼ cups sugar

2 tsp vanilla extract

½ tsp almond extract (optional)

¼ cup melted butter

¼ cup vegetable oil

½ cup whipping cream

½ cup milk

2 tbsp apple cider vinegar

1½ cups of the prepared Cherry Compote

ALMOND SHORTBREAD CRUMBLE

⅓ cup ground almonds

⅔ cup flour

⅓ cup butter

½ tsp vanilla extract

This delicious almond and vanilla flavoured treat has a sweet cherry compote swirled through the cake before being topped by a buttery almond shortbread crumble. I often bake this cake to take along to a brunch pot-luck, and most often it's the first thing to disappear.

> tip > The cherry compote will need to cool down before it can be used in this recipe, so make it first, or even a day or so ahead of when you plan to prepare the cake.

CHERRY COMPOTE

1. Simmer together the pitted cherries, sugar, and 3 tbsp water.

2. Stir together 1 ounce of water and the cornstarch. Add quickly to the simmering cherries, stirring constantly. Cook for only a minute before removing from heat and cooling to almost room temperature.

COFFEE CAKE

1. Sift together the flour and baking powder and set aside.

2. In the bowl of a stand mixer with the whisk attachment in place, whisk together on high speed the eggs, sugar, vanilla extract, and almond extract (optional) until the mixture is foamy and slightly stiffened.

3. Mix together the melted butter and vegetable oil in a measuring cup with a spout, then slowly add the oil and butter mixture to the egg mixture in a slow stream as the mixer continues to whisk.

4. Mix together the whipping cream, milk, and apple cider vinegar, and then add this slowly to the mixing bowl, continuing to mix but at a reduced speed.

5. Fold in the dry ingredients by hand with a rubber spatula, being careful not to over mix. Don't worry about lumps in the batter, they're fine.

6. Pour the batter into a greased and floured 10-inch springform pan. Dot the surface of the batter, a heaping tablespoon at a time, with the prepared Cherry Compote. Using the handle of a wooden spoon, swirl the cherry compote through the batter.

ALMOND SHORTBREAD CRUMBLE

1. Combine the ground almonds, flour, butter, and vanilla extract and pulse together in a food processor or rub the butter into the flour with your hands until fully incorporated.

2. Add the crumble topping to the surface of the coffee cake batter in the pan by squeezing together handfuls of the crumb mixture and breaking off small pieces. You can also add some slivered almonds and a few extra cherry pieces with the crumble for an extra flourish of garnish.

3. Bake for 50-60 minutes at 350°F or until a toothpick inserted in the center comes out clean. The toothpick test is definitely the best way to ensure this cake is fully baked. Cool in the pan for about 10 minutes before moving to a wire rack to cool completely, or serve warm after cooling for about 20 minutes.

Blueberry Crunch Muffins

Here's a twist on a real breakfast classic—the blueberry muffin. I've added a very crunchy oatmeal crumble baked right on top of the muffins for extra flavour and texture. The basic recipe makes amazingly moist and delicious plain blueberry muffins as well, if you prefer not to add the crumble. A sprinkle of turbinado sugar on top of the batter before baking is great on the plain muffins. And the base muffin batter is great for making other muffins like cranberry or raspberry too.

MAKES ABOUT 18 MUFFINS

BLUEBERRY MUFFINS

2½ cups flour

3 tsp baking powder

2 eggs

1¼ cups sugar

2 tsp vanilla extract

¼ cup melted butter

¼ cup vegetable oil

½ cup whipping cream

½ cup milk

2 tbsp apple cider vinegar

2 cups fresh or frozen blueberries

OATMEAL CRUNCH TOPPING

1 tsp baking powder

¾ cups oats (large)

1 cup flour

½ cup brown sugar

¾ cup butter, cut in small cubes

BLUEBERRY MUFFINS

1. Sift together the flour and baking powder and set aside.

2. In the bowl of a stand mixer with the whisk attachment in place, whisk together on high speed the eggs, sugar, and vanilla extract until foamy and slightly stiffened.

3. Mix together in a measuring cup with a spout the melted butter and vegetable oil.

4. Slowly add the oil and butter mixture to the egg mixture in a slow stream as the mixer continues to whisk.

5. Mix together the whipping cream, milk, and apple cider vinegar. Add slowly to the mixing bowl continuing to mix but at a reduced speed.

6. Fold in the dry ingredients by hand with a rubber spatula being careful not to over mix. Don't worry about lumps in the batter, they're fine. When the dry ingredients are almost incorporated, gently fold in the fresh or frozen blueberries.

7. Spoon the batter into well-greased muffin tins, filling them to the top.

OATMEAL CRUNCH TOPPING

1. Preheat the oven to 350°F. In a large bowl, toss together the baking powder, oats, flour, and brown sugar. Using your hands, rub the small cubes of butter thoroughly through the dry ingredients. Then sprinkle the crumble mixture evenly over the tops of the muffins.

2. Bake in the preheated oven for about 20-25 minutes or until a wooden toothpick inserted into the center of a muffin comes out clean. The baking time may vary depending on whether fresh or frozen berries are used.

Strawberry Chocolate Chip Buttermilk Pancakes

MAKES ABOUT **8–10** PANCAKES

1⅔ cups flour

½ tsp salt

3 tbsp sugar

3 tsp baking powder

½ tsp baking soda

1 egg

3 tsp vanilla extract

1½ cups buttermilk

4 tbsp melted butter

1½ cups chopped strawberries

½ cup chocolate chips

My daughter, Olivia, is the resident pancake expert and most often now takes the lead in whipping up a batch of these family favourite pancakes, especially when her friends are visiting for weekend sleepovers. She did a fantastic job on the batch in this photo and came up with the strawberry chocolate idea all on her own.

tip > Buttermilk makes for lighter pancakes because its natural acidity will more readily activate the baking powder or soda in pancake recipes. Always try not to over mix pancake batter. Stir it well but only just until the flour is fully incorporated. Never stir again after the initial mixing, or you risk denser pancakes. A few small lumps in pancake batter are never an issue either.

1. Sift together the flour, salt, sugar, baking powder, and baking soda, and set aside.

2. Whisk together the egg, vanilla extract, buttermilk, and melted butter. Pour this over the dry ingredients and whisk together just until combined. Do not over mix. Don't worry about small lumps. The batter will be thick.

3. Using a ¼ cup measure, pour batter onto a lightly greased griddle on medium-low heat; it's best to cook these slowly. You may need to spread the batter out a little with the back of a spoon.

4. Sprinkle chopped strawberries on the top, along with a sprinkle of chocolate chips. Cook for 3-4 minutes per side or until the center is fully cooked.

Crab Cakes Eggs Benedict

SERVES 4

CRAB CAKES

bread dough (for toutons) or substitute toasted English muffins

vegetable oil for frying

1 lb coarsely chopped (not minced) fresh or frozen cooked crab meat

¾ cup + 1 cup cracker crumbs

4 tbsp mayonnaise

1 tsp lemon zest, minced

2 tsp Worcestershire sauce

½ tsp salt

½ tsp pepper

2 tsp hot sauce (optional)

2 eggs, lightly beaten

approximately ⅔ cup canola oil for frying

HOLLANDAISE SAUCE

3 egg yolks

½ tsp yellow mustard (or Dijon if you prefer)

1-2 tbsp lemon juice

½ cup hot melted butter

½ tsp dry summer savoury (or dill or tarragon)

This brunch dish was inspired by a vacation road trip up the eastern seaboard of the US from Savannah to Boston. I tried some crab cake eggs Benedict along the way near Baltimore and knew I'd be making this dish with a bit of a Newfoundland twist.

Instead of an English muffin as the base, I've substituted traditional Newfoundland toutons, which are slowly fried white bread dough. Instead of the tarragon in the Hollandaise sauce, I use savoury, a favourite local herb.

CRAB CAKES

1. My crab cakes use only enough ingredients to hold the crab together, and the mixture will be quite soft when formed into cakes and then added to the cracker-crumb mixture. They do take a gentle touch, but once fried, they hold together quite well. Toasted English muffins or even my Best Buttermilk Biscuits recipe (see page 166) can replace the toutons if you prefer.

2. To prepare toutons, you can use store-bought pizza or bread dough if you like. Form the dough into 4-inch rounds about ¾ of an inch thick and let rise for 20 minutes before slowly frying them in vegetable oil until golden brown on both sides. Hold them in a warm oven until ready to assemble the Eggs Benedict.

3. Toss together the crab meat with the ¾ cup cracker crumbs and all other ingredients in the crab cakes except the canola oil. Divide in 4 portions and form into 3½ to 4-inch cakes. Roll each crab cake in additional cracker crumbs. Lay on a parchment-lined cookie sheet until ready to fry.

4. Heat about a ½ inch of canola oil in a skillet or sauté pan over medium-low heat. You want these to fry very gently. They will burn quickly if the oil is too hot. Fry until golden brown on both sides. Drain on paper towels.

HOLLANDAISE SAUCE

1. In a blender, combine the egg yolks, mustard, and lemon juice for only a few seconds.

2. With the blender on medium speed, slowly pour in the hot butter in a thin stream. The sauce should thicken quite quickly.

3. Stir in the savoury. Pour into a bowl and keep the bowl warm in a warm water bath while preparing the other components of the Eggs Benedict.

4. Place the cooked crab cakes on the warm toutons, top with a poached egg, and finally the Hollandaise sauce to serve.

Bacon Cheddar and Potato Frittata

SERVES 6

olive oil

3 cups diced roasted potatoes

½ lb crisp cooked bacon, chopped

½ lb aged cheddar cheese, diced

¼ cup chopped chives

10 large eggs

½ cup whipping cream

½ tsp salt

½ tsp pepper

½ tsp chili flakes (optional)

An easy-to-make frittata is a simple way to feed the brunch crowd without spending all morning in the kitchen, especially if you're using leftover or previously prepared ingredients such as leftover ham, sausage, or crisp cooked bacon. Frittatas also make excellent use of leftover plain pasta or potatoes. I've used leftover roasted potato nuggets in this frittata recipe prepared using the same method as in my Roast Potato recipe (see page 130), but any hash browns will do. Leftover plain rotini, farfalle, or fusilli pasta can also be substituted for the potatoes if that's what you have on hand.

1.   Preheat oven to 350°F. Heat a 12-inch oven-safe skillet on the stove. Brush a little olive oil on the bottom and sides of the skillet. When the skillet gets hot, remove it from the heat and sprinkle over the entire surface of the skillet, in even layers, the diced roasted potatoes, cooked bacon, cheddar, and chives.

2.   Quickly whisk together the eggs, whipping cream, salt, pepper, and chili flakes (optional).

3.   Bake in the preheated oven for about 25 minutes or until the eggs have set at the center. Serve immediately.

Bananas Foster French Toast

SERVES 4

FRENCH TOAST

4 eggs

⅓ cup whipping cream or milk

pinch of salt

1 tsp vanilla extract

8 slices of French bread (or 16 slices if using a smaller baguette)

BANANAS FOSTER SAUCE

6 tbsp butter

9 tbsp brown sugar

2 tsp vanilla extract

¼ cup rum

½ tsp cinnamon

¼ cup whipping cream

4 sliced bananas

Sometimes you can go all out with brunch and serve something that's practically dessert-like, and this recipe ideally fits that bill. I came up with this version for Spouse one year on Mother's Day. I prefer to use day-old crusty baguette because the extra crust provides great texture, and the little French toast pieces make for a beautiful presentation. It's a truly celebratory brunch idea.

FRENCH TOAST

1.   Whisk together the eggs, cream, salt, and vanilla. Let the bread soak in this mixture for a few minutes to absorb as much as possible. Fry in butter over medium-low heat until golden brown. You don't want to fry these too quickly.

BANANAS FOSTER SAUCE

1.   In a sauté pan, combine butter, brown sugar, vanilla extract, rum, and cinnamon. Cook over medium heat until the mixture is well incorporated and begins to get quite foamy. At that point, quickly whisk in the whipping cream.

2.   Immediately add the sliced bananas and cook for an additional minute, just until the bananas are warmed through. Be very careful as this sauce is very hot. Allow it to cool for a few minutes before serving over the prepared French toast.

Bread Pudding French Toast
with Mixed Berry Compote

SERVES 6–8

BREAD PUDDING

8-10 cups bread cubes (dense crusty bread works best for this recipe)

½ tsp freshly grated nutmeg

1 tsp cinnamon

2 cups whipping cream

2 cups milk

4 eggs

4 egg yolks

⅔ cup sugar

2 tbsp vanilla extract

pinch of salt

BUMBLEBERRY COMPOTE

4 cups fresh or frozen mixed berries (I use blueberries, raspberries, strawberries, and cherries)

¾ cup sugar

⅓ + ¼ cup water

1½ tbsp cornstarch

We are huge fans of bread pudding at our house, and you will find several bread pudding variations on my *Rock Recipes* website. Spouse in particular is very, very fond of bread pudding; that and Sticky Toffee Pudding (page 244) are her ultimate favourite desserts.

Leftover bread pudding baked in a loaf pan inspired this incredibily decadent brunch. I think this is an ideal idea if you're having guests for brunch because all the prep is done in advance, and all you have to do is take a few minutes to fry the pieces on a griddle when your guests arrive. Won't they be glad they got an invitation to brunch?

BREAD PUDDING

NOTE: Make these several hours in advance or even the day before.

1. Preheat oven to 350°F. Grease two loaf pans well. Toss the bread cubes with the grated nutmeg and cinnamon then pack the spiced bread cubes into the greased pans.

2. Whisk together whipping cream, milk, eggs, egg yolks, sugar, vanilla extract, and a pinch of salt until the sugar is dissolved. Pour the mixture evenly over the bread cubes, pressing down slightly to make sure all the cubes are soaked. Let sit on the countertop for 15 minutes to let the custard fully absorb into the bread.

3. Bake in the preheated oven for about 45-50 minutes until the custard is set and no longer liquid in the center. Cool completely before removing it from the pans, and chill completely in the fridge for several hours or overnight.

4. Slice the cold bread pudding in about 1-inch thick slices. Butter both sides of the slices and lightly fry to a golden brown on both sides before serving with powdered sugar and a topping of warm bumbleberry or other fruit compote.

BUMBLEBERRY COMPOTE

1. Combine the mixed berries, sugar, and ⅓ cup of water and bring to a gentle boil for 10 minutes. Thicken the compote with a slurry made by mixing together the cornstarch and ¼ cup of water. Add the slurry, stirring constantly, and cook for only an additional minute before removing from the heat. Cool for several minutes before serving over the fried bread pudding.

Easy Homemade Breakfast Sausage

I've recently started experimenting with making my own fresh sausages. I really love sausages, but I'm skeptical about the length of time some sausages spend in supermarket coolers. Seems there must be a lot of preservatives in there to give them the shelf life printed on the labels. Plus you're never sure what they're using for binders and fillers. They're almost always way too salty for my taste, and I just want to feel a little better about indulging in one of my favourite things to serve for weekend brunch.

Southern style breakfast sausage is one of my favourites, and I've worked on getting the seasoning just right in a good, easy, homemade version. I think this is it. Everyone loved this sausage, even the boy child who isn't a big fan of sausage in general. Be sure you have plenty of my Best Buttermilk Biscuits (recipe on page 166) on hand to serve with this tasty sausage. Make a larger batch to freeze for up to a couple of months, and enjoy these at brunch for several weekends to come.

MAKES ABOUT **12** PATTIES

2½ lbs ground pork shoulder or butt

1 tsp kosher salt

2 tsp smoked paprika

2 tsp brown sugar

1 tsp freshly ground black pepper

½ tsp chili flakes

½ tsp allspice

½ tsp nutmeg

2 tsp onion powder

1 tsp garlic powder

1 tsp marjoram (or oregano)

1 tsp ground sage

pinch of cayenne pepper (or more to taste)

1 tsp dry thyme

1. Cut the pork into small cubes. Mix the remaining ingredients together until well combined, and then toss the pork cubes in the spice mixture until they're completely coated.

NOTE: If you are using pre-ground pork, add it to a bowl a little at a time, sprinkling some of the spice mix between the layers before mixing together well. This ensures an even distribution of the spices throughout the sausage.

2. Coarsely grind the spiced pork cubes. Cover and place in the fridge for 1-2 hours or preferably overnight for the flavours to blend together. Form into 2 to 3-ounce patties and fry to lightly golden brown.

3. If freezing the sausage, place each patty between 2 pieces of parchment paper to more easily separate them when frozen. Stack a few at a time and wrap in plastic wrap or place in Ziploc bags to freeze.

Perfect Popovers *with* Peach Five-Spice Vanilla Jam

PERFECT POPOVERS (MAKES 12)

175 ml beaten egg, at room temperature

350 ml milk, at room temperature

350 ml sifted all-purpose flour

½ tsp salt

⅓ cup melted butter

PEACH FIVE-SPICE VANILLA JAM (MAKES ABOUT 2 CUPS)

6 large peaches, peeled and diced small

⅓ cup sugar

2 tsp vanilla extract, or the inside of one small vanilla pod

½ tsp Chinese five-spice powder

The perfect popover is not as difficult to achieve as many think, and I believe the absence of advice on good technique in many recipes out there is the reason this simple recipe fails so often for so many; after all, there are very few ingredients simply whisked together and baked, so what's the problem, right? Well I'd say careful measuring and careful preparation to create optimal conditions for the popovers to rise is the key.

Popover pans allow great circulation around the individual cups and undoubtedly add to the lightness of my popovers, but you can still get excellent results from a very generic set of muffin pans. One of the absolutely vital steps in the preparation of great popovers is preheating the pan in a very hot oven. This gives the popovers a great head start in rising as they don't have to wait for the pan to warm up in the oven. Do not pre-grease the pans with oil or butter when preheating them or you will quickly have a very smoky kitchen. Instead, I use melted butter poured into the bottoms of the muffin tins when they're hot and then very quickly brush it up the sides of the cups before pouring in the prepared batter. Using this method, and making sure your pans are very clean before starting, ensures the popovers will pop straight out of the pan without sticking...works for me every time.

It is extremely important that the batter for the popovers be at room temperature or even slightly warmer. I use lukewarm milk in my preparation and make very sure that my eggs are at room temperature. I sometimes even place the eggs in lukewarm water for 10 minutes to give them just a little extra temperature boost. A final tip for the batter is to measure carefully. A proper popover batter should have 2 parts flour and milk to 1 part egg volume. That is why I always measure my eggs. 3 extra large eggs typically produce about 175 ml in volume, but using different sized eggs will obviously yield different amounts. I've found that 175 ml of beaten egg with 350 ml each of sifted flour and milk produces the perfect amount of batter for 12 muffin tin-sized popovers.

The popover recipe is the same whether you are serving them with your favourite roast beef dinner or, as we love to do at our house, serve them at weekend brunch with some great seasonal fruit jam. One I love is this warm peach compote using amazing Ontario peaches with the added flavours of Chinese five-spice powder and fragrant, exotic vanilla. This combination of tender, crispy popovers and sweet, intense spiced peaches is delicious and will have you craving more by next weekend's brunch.

PERFECT POPOVERS

1. Preheat a 12-piece muffin pan in a 450°F oven.

2. Whisk together the eggs and milk. Sift together the flour and salt and make a well in the center. Pour the egg and milk mixture into the well and whisk together just until the liquid is incorporated. Small lumps are not a problem. Let the batter stand for 10 minutes. I like to make this batter in a bowl with a spout to make it easier and faster to pour into the prepared muffin pans, but if you don't have one, I recommend transferring the batter to a large measuring cup.

3. Working as quickly as you can so the pan does not cool down, pour the melted butter into the hot muffin tins to cover the bottom. Using a pastry brush, give it a quick brush up the sides of the muffin cups. Then quickly pour the batter evenly into the muffin pans. A ring of melted butter floating on the batter is normal and necessary at this point.

4. Quickly return the pan to the hot oven and bake for 15 minutes at 450°F before reducing the heat to 375°F and baking for an additional 15-20 minutes. The popovers should be a deep golden brown. It is *very, very* important not to open the oven door at any point in the baking time or you risk your popovers falling. Remove from oven and let rest for only a couple of minutes before removing them from the pan and serving.

PEACH FIVE-SPICE VANILLA JAM

1. Toss all the ingredients together in a medium saucepan and quickly simmer, stirring every few minutes until it reaches a thickened jam consistency. Serve warm with fresh popovers.

Chocolate Orange Coffee Cake

Regular readers of my *Rock Recipes* blog will not be surprised to see this flavour combination included in my brunch recipes. From profiteroles to trifles, anything that combines chocolate and orange is a well-established weakness of mine. I think it's perfectly acceptable to serve dessert at a brunch, particularly when it's the main meal of the day on a weekend. This delicious coffee cake, with its pound cake-like texture and upside-down crown of shimmering candied orange slices, is best served warm when it's at its fragrantly enticing best.

You will need to make the candied orange slices first so they can cool off a little before using them to line the cake pan.

SERVES 12

1 + 1½ cups sugar

1 + 1½ tsp vanilla extract or paste

½ cup water

2 thinly sliced oranges

1 cup butter

4 eggs

1¼ cups flour

1 cup cake flour

1½ tsp baking powder

¾ cup sour cream

¾ cup dark chocolate chips

1. In a non-stick saucepan, combine 1 cup of sugar, 1 tsp of vanilla extract or paste, and water. Bring to a slow boil until the sugar is dissolved, then add the orange slices.

2. Simmer slowly for about 10 minutes or until the liquid becomes syrupy, gently turning the orange slices over once during the cooking time. Grease a 9 or 10-inch round cake pan that is 2½-3 inches deep and line the bottom with a circle of parchment paper to help with the release of the cake later. Arrange the orange slices on the bottom of the pan and drizzle them with the syrup. Set aside to cool while you prepare the cake batter.

3. Preheat oven to 325°F.

4. Cream together well 1½ cups sugar, 1 cup of butter, and 1½ tsp vanilla. Add the eggs, one at a time, beating well after each addition.

5. Sift together the flour, cake flour, and baking powder, and then gently fold the dry ingredients, ⅓ at a time, into the creamed mixture alternately with sour cream.

6. Add the sour cream in 2 portions, so you begin and end the folding process with dry ingredients. With the last addition of dry ingredients, also fold in the chocolate chips.

7. Spread the batter evenly over the prepared orange slices in the pan.

8. Bake for about 1 hour or until a toothpick inserted in the center comes out clean. Cool on a wire rack for 15 minutes. Run a knife around the edge of the pan to ensure it doesn't stick and then invert the cake onto a serving plate.

suggestion > Delicious served warm with a dollop of freshly whipped cream.

Some of my earliest memories of making cookies as a child are of helping my mom with the annual marathon of Christmas baking that occurred at our house. For several days we would produce enough baked goods to feed a small army during the holiday season, filling the basement deep freezer to its fullest capacity.

Every year, there seemed to be a new recipe or two to go along with the old favourites, often collected from other avid bakers among family and friends. Those memories continue to inspire the sharing of great cookies, bars, and squares on *Rock Recipes*, particularly in the lead up to the holidays when these recipes take center stage on the blog.

While I do add cookie recipes during the year, my annual cookie obsession is no doubt the reason there are over 200 cookie recipes on *Rock Recipes* to date. It's a pretty impossible task to pick my best out of that many recipes, so I've relied heavily on reader favourites for these selections which turned out to be a pretty impressive collection.

Cookies *and* Bars

Nan Morgan's Snowballs

This recipe is virtually a Newfoundland icon. You'd be hard pressed to find anyone who's spent any time in this province and not sampled a Snowball. Someone in every family makes them, but my Nan Morgan's were always the best. More a confection than a cookie, a proper snowball should be soft, fudgy, and slightly chewy.

Key to the success of this recipe is the length of time that the base of the recipe is boiled. More precisely, the temperature the mixture reaches when boiling is critical. Akin to making fudge, you're looking for the mixture to reach soft ball stage or near soft ball stage on a candy thermometer. Use one if you have it, but if not, the five minutes gentle boiling as directed in the recipe is a pretty dependable guideline. It's also very important not to stir the mixture as it boils or you risk the sugar crystallizing and leaving you with a hard, crumbly finished product.

MAKES ABOUT 4 DOZEN

3 cups sugar

¾ cup melted butter

1¼ cups milk

3 cups large rolled oats

1 cup unsweetened dried fine coconut

¾ cup cocoa

1. In a large saucepan, combine the sugar, melted butter, and milk, and boil together gently over medium heat for 5 minutes or until the mixture reaches about 230°F on a candy thermometer.

2. Once mixture begins to boil, it's very important not to stir it at all.

3. Mix together the rolled oats, coconut, and cocoa. Add the boiled mixture to the dry ingredients and stir until well combined. Chill well for an hour or two in the fridge, stirring occasionally, until the mixture is able to be shaped into 1inch balls. Roll the balls in additional dried coconut.

tip > These should be stored in the fridge, and they freeze very well (my kids eat them frozen all the time, just like my siblings and I did when we were young).

Homemade Jammie Dodgers

A homemade version of what may be the most popular cookie in the British Isles, the Jammie Dodger. Wikipedia reports that 30% of the households there buy the commercially produced version of this cookie. It's basically just a simple, tender shortbread with raspberry jam, but its simplicity is also what makes it great. This may be the best "cuppa tea" cookie ever.

MAKES 10–12

2 cups flour

1 cup icing sugar (powdered sugar)

pinch of salt

1 cup + 2 tbsp cold butter, cut in cubes

2 large egg yolks

3 tsp vanilla extract

12-14 rounded tsp homemade or good quality raspberry jam (or whatever kind you like)

1. Sift together the flour, icing sugar, and salt. Set aside.

2. Rub the butter into the dry ingredients with your fingers until it's well incorporated and the mixture becomes crumbly, like a coarse meal.

3. Whisk together the egg yolks and vanilla extract, and then add them to the crumbly dry mixture and mix in until a soft dough forms. Wrap the dough in plastic wrap and chill in the fridge for at least 30 minutes.

4. Preheat oven to 350°F. Roll the dough out between two pieces of lightly floured parchment paper to about ⅛ of an inch thick. Cut out cookies using a 3-inch cutter and place on a parchment-lined baking sheet. Cut circles or hearts or whatever shape you like out of the centers of half of the cookies.

5. Bake in the preheated oven for 15-20 minutes, just until they start to brown slightly at the bottom edges but are still very pale. Remove from the oven and spoon 1 rounded teaspoon of your favourite good quality jam onto the middle of the bottom halves of the cookies, and spread out only slightly to about ¼ of an inch from the edge of the cookie. Carefully lay the top halves of the cookies onto the jam and press down lightly.

6. Return to the oven for an additional 5-6 minutes. This will heat up the jam to a point where it will stick the two cookie halves together.

7. Cool on the baking sheet for 10 minutes before transferring the cookies to a wire rack to cool completely. Store in airtight containers.

The Best Chocolate Chip Cookies

After many years of recipes and experiments, this is the final result of tweaking what I think is the perfect chocolate chip cookie. Soft and chewy with crispy edges and the perfect amount of rich chocolate morsels, I've never had better anywhere.

These days my kids have taken over the job of cookie baking for the most part, and either of them can turn out a mean batch of cookies all on their own from this outstanding recipe.

MAKES ABOUT 12 LARGE COOKIES

1⅓ cups all-purpose flour

½ tsp salt

½ tsp baking soda

½ cup butter

½ cup light brown sugar

½ cup white sugar

1 egg

1 tsp vanilla extract or butterscotch flavouring (or both! Hint, hint)

1 cup semisweet chocolate chips

1. Preheat oven to 350°F. Line cookie sheet(s) with parchment paper.

2. In a medium-sized bowl, whisk together flour, salt, and baking soda, and set aside.

3. In a large bowl, cream together the butter and sugars until light and fluffy. Add the egg and vanilla and combine thoroughly. Then add the flour mixture to the creamed mixture. Mix only enough to incorporate the flour. Do not over mix. Fold in the chocolate chips.

4. Form cookies by dropping rounded teaspoons of dough, two inches apart, on the prepared cookie sheet.

5. Bake in the preheated oven until light brown around the edges, about 12-15 minutes, depending on cookie size.

6. Over baking is the biggest problem with most chocolate chip cookies. Your oven temperature and the type of cookie sheet you use will vary the baking times considerably. When they are golden brown around the edges, it's time to remove them from the oven. Thinking they are a little underdone is probably a good thing. Experiment by baking only a couple of cookies at a time to see what the perfect baking time is for your oven.

7. Cool for 10 minutes on the baking sheet before removing to a wire rack to cool thoroughly.

Nutella Fudge Crumble Bars

MAKES ABOUT 30 COOKIE BARS

NUTELLA FUDGE FILLING

1 cup chocolate chips

½ cup whipping cream (or evaporated milk)

1 cup Nutella

1 cup icing sugar (powdered sugar, confectioner's sugar)

CRUMBLE BARS

2 tsp baking powder

2 cups rolled oats (large)

2 cups flour

1 cup brown sugar

1½ cups butter, cut in small cubes

Crumble bars have been a favourite of mine since childhood. As a beginner baker when I was still a child, I remember experimenting with the filling for the iconic Newfoundland favourite Date Crumbles, adding many different fillings from blueberry to apple to apricot, and that experimental inspiration hit me again with this delicious recipe including everyone's favourite, Nutella. The result was amazing! The kids absolutely love them and Spouse, who normally can show great restraint, has more than her fair share when these get baked at home.

NUTELLA FUDGE FILLING

1. In a double boiler, melt the chocolate chips, whipping cream, and Nutella together until smooth. Don't let this mixture get too hot. As soon as the chocolate is melted, take it off the heat. Then add the icing sugar and blend in until smooth.

CRUMBLE BARS

1. Preheat oven to 350°F. In a large bowl, toss together the baking powder, rolled oats, flour, and brown sugar. Then, using your hands, rub the butter thoroughly through the dry ingredients. This mixture should hold together when squeezed in your fist.

2. Divide the crumble mixture in half and press half into the bottom of a 9x13-inch greased or parchment-lined baking pan. Spread the Nutella Fudge Filling mixture over the base. Top with remaining crumb mixture, breaking it into small pieces with your fingers. Bake in the preheated oven for 40 minutes or until golden brown.

3. Cool completely on a wire rack before cutting into bars or squares.

tip > When making cookie-bar recipes, always line the bottom and the 2 longest sides of the greased pan with a single sheet of parchment paper that's been cut to fit. The paper should extend above the sides of the pan by about 1-2 inches. When the cookie bars have baked and completely cooled, run a sharp knife along the 2 shorter unlined sides then use the ends of the parchment paper to lift the entire batch out of the pan. This allows you to place the cookie bars on a flat surface, making it far easier to cut them neatly and evenly.

Chocolate Chip Cookie Dough Cheesecake Bars

For many, this will be the holy grail of cookie bars: a perfect caloric storm of flavour with a buttery graham cracker crumb crust, a vanilla cheesecake center, and gobs of cookie dough on top. Because the cookie dough gets baked on top of the cheesecake, it just bakes to a light golden colour on top and retains a cookie dough texture underneath. What an amazing combination in a single treat! They also freeze very well, so you can take one or two out at a time to enjoy over several weeks...if they last that long.

MAKES 2 DOZEN BAR COOKIES

GRAHAM CRACKER CRUMB CRUST
1½ cups graham cracker crumbs

⅓ cup melted butter

2 tbsp sugar

VANILLA CHEESECAKE CENTER
1 cup cream cheese (8 oz package)

⅓ cup sugar

1 egg

1 tsp vanilla extract

COOKIE DOUGH TOPPING
⅓ cup butter

¼ cup white sugar

¼ cup dark brown sugar

1 tsp vanilla extract

¾ cup flour

pinch of salt

⅔ cup chocolate chips

GRAHAM CRACKER CRUMB CRUST

1. Preheat oven to 325°F. Mix together the graham cracker crumbs, melted butter, and sugar. Press firmly into the bottom of a greased or parchment-lined 9x9-inch baking pan. Bake for 5 minutes in the preheated oven.

VANILLA CHEESECAKE CENTER

1. Cream together very well the cream cheese and sugar. Then add the egg and vanilla extract. Mix until well blended. Spread evenly over the graham crumb crust.

COOKIE DOUGH TOPPING

1. Preheat oven to 325°F.

2. Cream together very well the butter, white sugar, brown sugar, and vanilla extract. Fold in the flour and salt just until a dough forms. Finally, mix in the chocolate chips.

3. Pick up the cookie dough in handfuls and press into a ball. Break off small nuggets of the dough and sprinkle these evenly over the cheesecake layer.

4. Bake in the preheated oven for 30-35 minutes or until the cookie dough just begins to brown on top. Cool completely in the pan before cutting into squares or bars. If you're not freezing these cookie bars, store in an airtight container in the fridge.

Queen Anne Squares

MAKES ABOUT 2 DOZEN

BOTTOM LAYER

⅔ cup melted butter

⅔ cup brown sugar

1 cup flour

4 tbsp cocoa

1 tsp vanilla extract

1 extra-large egg (or 1½ medium)

COCONUT LAYER

1 can sweetened condensed milk

2 cups dried coconut

1 tsp vanilla extract

CHOCOLATE FROSTING

2 cups icing sugar (powdered sugar)

3 tbsp cocoa

1 tsp vanilla

2 or 3 tbsp milk

¼ cup butter

These delicious cookie squares are a local favourite in Newfoundland, and you can find them in many local bakeries. I developed my own version of this popular treat, modifying it to make the moist cake base a little thicker to better support the delicious coconut filling and chocolate frosting top. The final result reminds me of a chocolate and coconut candy bar in soft, moist, cookie-bar form.

BOTTOM LAYER

1. Beat together the melted butter, brown sugar, flour, cocoa, vanilla extract, and egg until smooth. Then spread evenly into the bottom of a lightly greased and parchment paper-lined 9x9-inch baking pan.

COCONUT LAYER

1. Preheat oven to 350°F. Mix together the condensed milk, coconut, and vanilla extract until completely blended then drop by heaping teaspoonfuls onto the cake batter layer. Spread out carefully. Bake in the preheated oven for 25 minutes. Cool completely before adding the chocolate frosting on top.

CHOCOLATE FROSTING

1. Beat together the icing sugar, cocoa, vanilla, milk, and butter until smooth. Add only enough milk to bring the frosting to a smooth but spreadable consistency. A frosting that is a bit on the thick consistency side works best here. Spread on the cooled cookies and cut into squares or bars.

Orange Dark Chocolate Chip Cookies

MAKES ABOUT 2 DOZEN

1¼ cups butter

2 cups sugar

2 large eggs

1 tbsp vanilla extract

¾ cup cocoa powder

2 cups flour

1 tsp baking soda

½ tsp salt

zest of 1 large orange, finely minced

1½ cups chocolate chips

Yes, I know, another chocolate orange combination, but this is a fantastic, chewy, crispy edged cookie made from a rich cocoa dough with dark chocolate chips and fragrant orange zest. For fans of the popular Terry's Chocolate Orange, trust me, this is going to be your favourite cookie!

> tip > Using parchment paper on cookie sheets regularly can prevent cookies from burning. Greasing cookie sheets with butter or spray oil can cause a dark brown build up on the pans over time, and this build up can cause heat to be conducted too quickly. I always use aluminum cookie sheets lined with parchment paper for perfect drop or cut-out cookies every time.

NOTE: The dough needs to be very cold, so start these cookies the day before.

1. Cream together the butter and sugar. Add the eggs and vanilla extract to the creamed mixture and beat until well combined.

2. Sift together the cocoa, flour, baking soda, and salt. Add the dry ingredients to the creamed mixture along with the chocolate chips and orange zest. Mix well until a dough forms.

3. Wrap the dough in plastic wrap and refrigerate for several hours or overnight. Dough must be very cold when it goes in the oven.

4. Preheat oven to 350°F. Roll into 1-inch balls. Place about 2 inches apart on a parchment paper-lined baking sheet and bake in preheated oven for about 8-10 minutes. Allow the cookies to cool on the pan for several minutes before placing them on a wire rack to cool completely.

Lemon Coconut Crumble Bars

This is a very old family recipe of mine, but I have often seen them in local bakeries across Newfoundland. There are versions without the coconut, but we always had them with coconut in our family. While some use a packaged lemon pie filling in their versions, I like to make my own from scratch. This recipe works well with other citrus fruits like orange and lime as well.

MAKES ABOUT 36 BARS

LEMON FILLING

⅓ cup cornstarch

⅓ cup cake flour

pinch of salt

1½ cups sugar

2 cups water

5 egg yolks, slightly beaten

zest of 2 large (or 3 small) lemons, very finely chopped

juice of 2 large (or 3 small) lemons

3 tbsp butter

LEMON COCONUT CRUMBLE BARS

2 cups flour

¾ cup sugar

1 tsp baking powder

2 cups dried coconut, medium cut

pinch of salt

1 cup butter, cut in small pieces

LEMON FILLING

1. Combine the cornstarch, salt, cake flour, sugar, and water in a medium saucepan. Cook over medium-low heat until the mixture thickens, stirring constantly. Remove from heat.

2. Pour about ½ cup of the thickened mixture over the beaten egg yolks and whisk together quickly. This tempers the egg yolks so they don't scramble.

3. Pour this mixture back into the pot and whisk it in quickly. Return the pot to the heat and stir constantly for a few minutes until the mixture is thick and evenly smooth.

4. Whisk in the lemon juice and zest and remove from the heat. Finally, whisk in the butter and set aside to cool while you prepare the crumble mixture.

LEMON COCONUT CRUMBLE BARS

1. Preheat oven to 350°F. Sift together the flour, sugar, baking powder, coconut, and salt. Using your hands or a pastry blender, cut in the butter until it's completely incorporated into the dry ingredients.

2. Press half of the crumb mixture into the bottom of a 9x13-inch, well-greased baking pan. Pour the lemon filling evenly over the bottom crumbs. Gently sprinkle the remaining crumbs over the lemon filling and press down gently.

3. Bake in the preheated oven for 40-45 minutes or until light golden brown in colour. Cool completely in the pan before cutting into squares and serving.

Millionaire Pecan Praline Bars

MAKES ABOUT **2** DOZEN

MILLIONAIRE PECAN PRALINE BARS

1 cup butter

1½ cup brown sugar

2 eggs

2 tsp vanilla extract

2 cups flour

1 tsp baking powder

¼ tsp baking soda

PRALINE CARAMEL

¾ cup butter

¾ cup dark brown sugar

2 tsp vanilla extract

one 10 oz can of sweetened condensed milk

1½ cups lightly toasted pecans

I often get cookie recipes suggested to me by followers of *Rock Recipes*. Sometimes though, I just receive a description or a photo of a cookie that someone has sampled, and since they don't have the recipe, they ask that I try to replicate it. This one was suggested as a sort of Millionaire shortbread but with a soft cookie base. The caramel was described as soft and rich with more of a praline flavour. Finally, instead of a chocolate top, there were toasted pecans. This recipe was the result of cobbling together and tweaking elements from several of my old standard cookie recipes and, if I do say so myself, with a very delicious result. I liked it so much, in fact, I held it in reserve to feature as a brand new cookie bar recipe for this book.

MILLIONAIRE PECAN BARS

1. Preheat oven to 350°F or 325°F if using glass bake ware. Grease a 9x9-inch baking pan and line it with parchment paper. I always line cookie pans with parchment paper so I can lift the entire batch of cookies out and cut them on a cutting board rather than the more difficult method of trying to cut them evenly while still in the pan. They will always look better when cut on a board and your pans will not have scraped bottoms.

2. Cream together the butter and brown sugar. Then beat in the eggs and vanilla extract.

3. Sift together the flour, baking powder, and baking soda. Fold the dry ingredients into the creamed mixture and spread evenly into the prepared pan.

4. Bake for 40 minutes. Cool completely on a wire rack before making the praline caramel layer.

PRALINE CARAMEL

1. In a small saucepan, melt the butter, and then add the brown sugar and vanilla extract. Stir until the brown sugar is dissolved then add the sweetened condensed milk.

2. Slowly simmer this mixture, stirring constantly until the mixture reaches soft ball stage, 235°F on a candy thermometer. You can also test for soft ball stage by dropping a teaspoon of the mixture into ice water where it should cool quickly into a ball that is soft enough to pinch between your thumb and forefinger.

3. Remove the caramel from the heat and pour over the prepared cookie base. Be very careful, this mixture is very hot. Let it cool at room temperature for 15 minutes or so before topping with lightly toasted pecans. Lightly press the pecans into the caramel with the back of a spoon. Cool completely in the fridge for a few hours before cutting into squares or bars.

I started baking cakes from scratch before I was even a teenager.
Growing up, we always baked cherry pound cakes, boiled raisin cakes, and other fruitcakes from scratch for special occasions and especially Christmas, but cake mixes were more the norm for the rest of the year. I had already been baking for years when I started occasionally getting cookbooks as gifts, and there began my quest to collect, tweak, and even completely create my own scratch cake recipes.

This collection is a good cross section of what I've learned over the years about baking a great cake and some excellent choices for any celebration or just a plain old Sunday dinner dessert.

Cakes

Red Velvet Cake

This Red Velvet Cake is a hybrid recipe taking its inspiration from several versions of this classic southern dessert cake that I've tried over the years. In general, I've found that the simpler the recipe, the better the cake. This recipe really could not be simpler; it just mixes the wet ingredients and dry ingredients separately and then brings them together to form a very pourable batter, which produces a very moist cake.

SERVES 12–16

DOUBLE CREAM CHEESE FROSTING

1½ cups (12 oz) **cream cheese**

¾ cup **butter**

2 tsp **vanilla extract**

1 kilo bag of **icing sugar** (about 8 cups)

1-3 tbsp **milk**; enough to bring the frosting to a spreadable consistency

RED VELVET CAKE

1¼ cups **all-purpose flour**

1¼ cups **cake flour**

1½ cups **sugar**

½ tsp **baking soda**

1½ tsp **baking powder**

1 tsp **salt**

3 tbsp **cocoa**

1 cup **vegetable oil**

1½ cups **buttermilk**

2 large **eggs**

1½ tsp liquid **red food colouring**

1½ tsp **white vinegar**

2 tsp **vanilla extract**

1 cup chopped **toasted pecans**

DOUBLE CREAM CHEESE FROSTING

1. Mix all the ingredients together and beat well until smooth and fluffy.

RED VELVET CAKE

1. Grease two 9-inch cake pans and line the bottom and sides with parchment paper. Preheat oven to 325°F.

2. Sift together the all-purpose flour, cake flour, sugar, baking soda, baking powder, salt, and cocoa, and set aside.

3. In the bowl of an electric mixer, blend together well the vegetable oil, buttermilk, eggs, red food colouring, white vinegar, and vanilla extract. Then mix in the dry ingredients all at once and blend until smooth. Do not over mix the batter. As soon as there are no lumps in the batter, pour into the prepared cake pans.

4. Bake in the preheated oven for 30-35 minutes or until a wooden toothpick inserted in the center comes out clean.

5. Turn cakes onto a wire rack, remove the parchment paper, and cool completely. When the cake is completely cool, you can cut the 2 layers into 4 using a sharp serrated bread knife, if you like, or just use 2 layers if you prefer. I think the 4 layers achieves a good ratio of cake to frosting in each bite.

6. Fill all of the layers and the top of the cake with Double Cream Cheese Frosting, sprinkling each layer with ¼ cup of the toasted pecans.

note > I've seen some recipes that include an outrageous amount of red food colouring, which I am not particularly fond of using in general. This recipe uses a very reasonable 1½ tsp of liquid red food colouring. Recipes also vary greatly on the amount of cocoa in a Red Velvet Cake, ranging from only a teaspoon to several tablespoons. I prefer the higher end of the cocoa scale for just a little more chocolate edge to this terrific cake. Some folks object to this because it produces a more brownish red cake, so if this is a concern, you can cut back on the cocoa. But don't omit it altogether; the red velvet purists will hunt you down for that crime against cake!

Caramel Cake

I've often tasted caramel cake on road trips in the southern states, and they almost always look rustic and homemade, often with the caramel just poured over the cake in a simple but appealing presentation. I wanted to make one that looked a little more polished to maybe use as a celebration cake for a birthday or anniversary dinner. This one worked out quite well. The moist vanilla cake gets filled with layers of homemade caramel sauce then covered in a caramel buttercream frosting and drizzled with a little more caramel sauce. Be warned that this cake is utterly delicious and irresistible to caramel lovers, but it's intentionally very rich, and small slices are more than satisfying. This cake will serve up to twice as many folks as other layer cakes, which makes it ideal for a great celebration.

SERVES 16–20

CARAMEL SAUCE (SEE PAGE 240)

CARAMEL FROSTING
3½-4 cups icing sugar
(powdered sugar)

½ cup butter

2 tsp vanilla extract

½ cup caramel sauce
(recipe on page 240)

a few tbsp milk

VANILLA CAKE
1¼ cups sifted all-purpose flour

1¼ cups sifted cake flour

½ tsp baking soda

2 tsp baking powder

1 tsp salt

½ cup butter

2 tbsp good quality vanilla extract

1½ cups sugar

½ cup vegetable oil

3 large eggs

1¼ cups milk

CARAMEL SAUCE (SEE PAGE 240)

CARAMEL FROSTING
1. Beat all ingredients together until smooth and fluffy with a spreadable consistency. Use a couple of tablespoons of milk to begin, and add more if need be. If it becomes too thin, just add a couple more tablespoons of icing sugar at a time.

VANILLA CAKE
1. Grease two 8-inch or 9-inch cake pans and line the bottoms with parchment paper. Preheat oven to 325°F.

2. Sift together the all-purpose flour, cake flour, baking soda, baking powder, and salt, and set aside.

3. In the bowl of an electric mixer with the whisk attachment, beat together well, at high speed, the butter, vanilla extract, and sugar until the mixture is light and fluffy. Then slowly beat in the vegetable oil. Next, beat in the eggs one at a time. Fold in the dry ingredients alternately while adding the milk.

4. I always add dry ingredients in 3 divisions and liquid ingredients in 2 divisions. It's very important to begin and end the additions with the dry ingredients. Do not over mix the batter. As soon as the batter has no lumps, pour into the two prepared cake pans.

5. Bake in the preheated oven for 30-35 minutes or until a wooden toothpick inserted in the center comes out clean. Allow the cake to cool in the pans for 10 minutes before turning out onto wire racks to cool completely.

6. To construct the cake, cut the 2 layers into 4. Reserve about ⅔ cup of the caramel sauce (½ cup for the frosting and the rest to drizzle on top of the cake). Divide the remaining caramel sauce into 3 parts and use it to fill the three inner layers of the cake. Frost with the caramel frosting and drizzle with any remaining caramel sauce.

Black and White Cake

There's no counting the number of Black and White Cakes I have made over the years. Most often these days, my kids like to make them on their own with a little help from dear old Dad when preparing the frosting.

As you can imagine, a chocolate scratch cake with a marshmallow type frosting is a big kid favourite and has been made for countless children's parties where even crumbs are hard to come by afterward. More than a few adults I know love it as much as the kids. When it comes to standard recipes at our house, this one is unquestionably in the top ten.

SERVES 16–20

CHOCOLATE CAKE

2 cups **sugar**

2 cups **all-purpose flour**

¾ cup **cocoa**

2 tsp **baking powder**

1 tsp **baking soda**

½ tsp **salt**

2 **eggs**

1 cup **soured milk** (1 tbsp lemon juice or white vinegar plus milk to measure 1 cup total)

1 cup **black coffee** (additional milk can be substituted if you prefer)

½ cup **vegetable oil**

1 tsp **vanilla extract**

MARSHMALLOW FROSTING

1¼ cups **sugar**

½ cup **corn syrup**

¼ cup **water**

4 **egg whites**

¼ tsp **cream of tarter**

2 tsp **vanilla extract**

CHOCOLATE CAKE

1. Preheat the oven to 350°F. Grease and flour two 8-inch or 9-inch cake pans. I also like to line the bottoms of the pans with circles of parchment paper to ensure an easy release after baking.

2. Combine all ingredients in a mixing bowl and beat with an electric mixer for 2 minutes.

3. Pour the batter into the prepared cake pans, and bake in the preheated oven for 30-35 minutes or until a toothpick inserted in the center comes out clean. Cool completely.

MARSHMALLOW FROSTING

1. In a small saucepan, combine sugar, corn syrup, and water. Bring to a boil over medium heat and continue to cook until the mixture reaches 240°F on a candy thermometer or when a teaspoonful of the mixture dropped into ice water forms a soft ball that holds its shape when cool.

2. Whip the egg whites, cream of tartar, and vanilla extract to soft peaks in a large bowl. With the mixer on medium-high speed, slowly begin to pour the sugar syrup down the side of the egg-white bowl in a thin continuous stream. Continue to whip the frosting until it forms stiff peaks.

3. Frost your cake immediately with this frosting while it is still slightly warm as it is easier to spread smoothly than if allowed to cool completely.

Mango Ginger Carrot Cake *with* Candied Ginger Cream Cheese Frosting

SERVES 12–16

MANGO GINGER CARROT CAKE

2 cups **flour**

1 tsp **baking powder**

1 tsp **baking soda**

2 tsp **cinnamon**

¾ tsp freshly grated **nutmeg**

2 tsp **powdered ginger**

½ tsp **salt**

1½ cups **sugar**

3 **eggs** lightly beaten

2 tsp **vanilla extract**

1 cup **vegetable oil**

1½ cups **grated carrots**

1 cup **fresh ripe mango**, diced small

2 tbsp finely grated **fresh ginger root**

½ cup chopped **lightly toasted macadamia nuts** (optional)

CREAM CHEESE GINGER FROSTING

½ cup **cream cheese**

½ cup **butter**

2 tsp **vanilla extract**

2 tbsp **candied ginger** (packed in syrup), very finely minced

5 cups **icing sugar** (powdered sugar)

1-3 tbsp **milk** (or ginger syrup from the candied ginger); only enough to bring the frosting to a spreadable consistency

I love mangoes and Spouse loves ginger, so when thinking up a new version of carrot cake, we combined the two flavours into this incredibly moist and delicious dessert. A perfect marriage of flavours...just like us! The candied ginger in the cream cheese frosting gives it a little extra zing too.

MANGO GINGER CARROT CAKE

1. Preheat oven to 325°F. Grease and flour two 8-inch or 9-inch cake pans.

2. Sift together flour, baking powder, baking soda, cinnamon, nutmeg, powdered ginger, and salt, and set aside.

3. In a large mixing bowl, beat the sugar, eggs, vanilla, and oil until light and fluffy. Stir in the grated carrots, mango, grated ginger root, and nuts (if you're using them).

4. Fold in the dry ingredients by hand. Stir only until the dry ingredients are incorporated into the batter. Do not over mix.

5. Pour into the prepared pans and bake for 30-35 minutes or until a wooden toothpick inserted into the center of the cake comes out clean.

CREAM CHEESE GINGER FROSTING

1. Mix all the ingredients together and beat very well until smooth and fluffy. Add the milk or ginger syrup last to get the frosting to the right consistency.

2. If you can't find candied ginger, simply simmer gently ½ cup sugar and ½ cup water with peeled ginger slices in a small saucepan for about 20 minutes or until the liquid thickens to a clear syrupy consistency. Watch this carefully because it can burn quickly.

Rum Truffle Cake

This is quite a simple cake but elegant and impressive at the same time. I start with a light, airy sponge cake that gets soaked with a little rum before being filled and covered with an easy to make chocolate rum truffle and whipped ganache frosting. So luscious!

SERVES 10–12

SPONGE CAKE

1 cup **flour**

1 tsp **baking powder**

6 **eggs** separated, room temperature

¼ tsp **cream of tartar**

1 cup **sugar**, separated in 2 half cups

2 tsp **vanilla extract**

½ tsp **lemon flavouring** (optional)

4 oz **dark rum**

CHOCOLATE RUM TRUFFLE WHIPPED GANACHE FROSTING

3 cups **dark chocolate chips**

½ + 2 cups **whipping cream**

2 oz **dark rum**

SPONGE CAKE

1. Preheat the oven to 325°F. Line the bottoms of two 8-inch pans with circles of parchment paper but leave the pans ungreased.

2. Sift together and set aside the flour and baking powder.

3. For the meringue base of the batter, you will need the eggs (yolks and whites separated), cream of tartar, 2 half-cups of sugar, vanilla extract, and lemon flavouring.

4. Beat the egg whites and cream of tartar until foamy. Add ½ cup sugar gradually until egg whites are stiff.

5. In a separate bowl, beat the egg yolks and ½ cup sugar until foamy and thickened.

6. Fold the beaten egg yolks into the beaten egg whites along with the vanilla (and lemon) for only a few turns. Then, using a rubber spatula, slowly and gradually fold in the flour and baking powder mixture very gently *by hand* until just incorporated into the meringue mixture. I mix in the dry ingredients in 3 equal portions. Do not over mix, you just want the flour to be incorporated; over mixing will deflate the egg whites and result in a tough-textured final product.

7. Spread the batter evenly into the 8-inch round cake pans that have the bottoms lined with parchment paper and bake in the preheated oven for 25-30 minutes or until center springs back when touched. Cool completely in the pans.

8. When the cake is completely cooled, run a sharp knife around the edge of the pans to release the cake and remove the parchment paper circles from the bottoms. Split the 2 layers into 4 using a sharp serrated knife and sprinkle *each layer* with 1 oz rum.

CHOCOLATE RUM TRUFFLE WHIPPED GANACHE FROSTING

1. To prepare the frosting, melt together the chocolate chips and ½ of cup whipping cream in a double boiler. Stir constantly over a gentle simmer until just melted and smooth throughout. You do not want this mixture to get hot. It should be just at the melting point and only lukewarm to the touch.

2. Transfer to a large mixing bowl and stir in the rum.

3. In a separate bowl, whip the 2 cups of whipping cream to firm peaks. Then add the whipped cream to the chocolate mixture in four portions, folding gently after each addition until the whipped cream is completely incorporated into the chocolate.

4. At this point, you will probably have to chill this frosting for 30 minutes or so in the fridge if it is too soft to work with. Just give it a quick, gentle fold with a rubber spatula every 10 minutes so that it cools evenly in the fridge.

5. Fill and frost the rum-soaked cake layers with the frosting and garnish with fresh berries if desired. Chill the cake for at least a couple of hours before serving.

Vanilla Cream Cheese Bundt Cake

SERVES 10–12

VANILLA CREAM CHEESE BUNDT CAKE

1½ cups sugar

8 oz cream cheese (one standard Philadelphia brand block)

1 cup butter

3 tsp pure vanilla extract

4 eggs

1¼ cups flour

1 cup cake flour

1½ tsp baking powder

VANILLA CREAM CHEESE GLAZE

2 cups icing sugar (powdered sugar)

4 oz cream cheese (½ a standard Philadelphia brand block)

1 tsp pure vanilla extract

2-3 tsp milk

Vanilla lovers are much quieter by nature. They don't need to constantly shout about their flavour passion like some chocolate lovers do (Oops! Points finger at self). This recipe is for those quiet vanilla fans out there. And I hope they'll enjoy the added richness and flavour that cream cheese brings to a cake batter.

This cake recipe can also be baked in two loaf pans if you don't have a Bundt pan, but it may be time to invest in one if you don't; this recipe baked up absolutely perfectly in my pan.

VANILLA CREAM CHEESE BUNDT CAKE

1. Preheat oven to 325°F. Cream together well the sugar, cream cheese, butter, and vanilla extract. Then add the eggs, one at a time.

2. Separately, sift together the flour, cake flour, and baking powder. Then gently fold the dry ingredients into the creamed mixture until the flour is fully incorporated.

3. Bake in a well-greased and floured Bundt pan (or two parchment-lined loaf pans) in the preheated oven for about 50-60 minutes or until a toothpick inserted in the center comes out clean. Let the cake rest in the pan for 5-10 minutes before turning it out onto a wire rack to cool completely, then frost with Vanilla Cream Cheese Glaze.

VANILLA CREAM CHEESE GLAZE

1. Beat all ingredients together very well in an electric mixer until very smooth. Add more or less milk to get the glaze to the proper consistency, which should be relatively thick but not quite pourable. Spoon and swirl the glaze on top of the cake and let it drip down naturally.

Blueberry Snack Cake

I cannot count the number of times I've made this simple, moist, delicious, buttery little snack cake with an abundance of wild Newfoundland blueberries baked right in. A terrific addition to any brown-bag lunch, it's indeed a blueberry snack cake, but we often had it as a duff with Sunday dinner when I was a kid here in Newfoundland. Sometimes we still do. I often substitute local partridgeberries or bakeapples (lingonberries or cloudberries) to make other delicious versions. I've also used one of my favourites, fresh raspberries, with great success. I love the way fruits like raspberries leave little jammy pockets in the cake. Raisins are another popular substitution for the blueberries, but your favourite dried fruit, like apricots or cherries, would be delicious too; just be sure to cut them small enough; about the size of large raisins is about right.

This humble little blueberry cake also dresses up nicely as a luscious comfort-food dessert when served warm from the oven with warm vanilla custard.

SERVES 9

½ cup **butter**

¾ cup **sugar**

2 **eggs**

2 tsp **vanilla extract**

2 cups **flour**

2 tsp **baking powder**

1 cup **milk**

1½ cups **fresh** or **frozen blueberries**

1. Preheat oven to 325°F. Grease a 9x9-inch baking pan well.

2. Cream together the butter and sugar until light and fluffy. Then add the eggs (one at a time) and vanilla extract. Beat well after the addition of each egg.

3. Sift together the flour and baking powder. Add the dry ingredients to the creamed mixture alternately with the milk. Always begin and end with an addition of dry ingredients. As a general rule, add the flour mixture in three divisions and the milk in two.

4. Quickly fold in the fresh or frozen blueberries, and spread the batter evenly into the prepared pan.

5. Bake in the preheated oven for about 40-45 minutes or until a toothpick inserted in the center comes out clean. The baking time can vary, especially if you use frozen berries. In that case, it may take 10 or even 15 minutes more to bake. The toothpick test is the best way to ensure this cake is fully baked.

Chocolate Soufflé Cake *with* Irish Cream Whipped Cream and Caramel Drizzle: A Gluten Free Recipe

SERVES 12–16

CHOCOLATE SOUFFLÉ CAKE

1 cup **unsalted butter**

1 lb **dark chocolate**, chopped (at least 50% cocoa)

1 tsp **vanilla**

½ cup **cocoa**

½ tsp **fine salt**

10 extra-large **eggs**, room temperature

¾ cup **sugar** (divided into ½ and ¼ cup)

CARAMEL SAUCE (SEE PAGE 240)

IRISH CREAM WHIPPED CREAM

2 cups **whipping cream**

4 rounded tbsp **icing sugar** (powdered sugar)

⅓ cup **Bailey's Irish Cream Liqueur**

I first made this cake for a friend's birthday celebration, and it was a *huge* hit. It's a pretty simple recipe too, and no, there's no mistake: this is a flour-less cake, which makes it a great gluten-free cake as well. But there's no need to disclose that fact because, with its deep chocolate flavour and melt-in-your-mouth texture, nobody will care.

The Irish cream flavoured whipped cream contrasts nicely with the dark chocolate cake, and I like to drizzle the cake with Caramel Sauce (recipe page 240) as well while serving some on the side in case folks would like a little extra…and folks always want a little extra!

CHOCOLATE SOUFFLÉ CAKE

1. Preheat oven to 350°F. Grease two 9-inch cake pans and dust with cocoa. Line the bottoms with parchment paper to easily release the cake when baked.

2. Melt the butter and chocolate in a double boiler just until melted. Set aside to cool almost to room temperature then stir in the cocoa, vanilla, and salt until smooth.

3. Separate the eggs and beat the whites to soft peaks. Slowly beat in the ½ cup of sugar to form a meringue. Transfer to a large mixing bowl. Beat the egg yolks and ¼ cup of sugar until light and foamy and fold into the meringue along with the chocolate mixture. A gentle touch is needed here so as not to deflate the meringue too much.

4. Divide the batter equally into the cake pans and bake in the preheated oven for about 30 minutes or until the centers of the cakes spring back when lightly touched. Cool in the pans for about 20 minutes before removing them from the pan and cooling completely on a wire rack. NOTE: This cake will fall somewhat in the pans as it cools, and this is perfectly normal for this recipe.

CARAMEL SAUCE (SEE PAGE 240)

IRISH CREAM WHIPPED CREAM

1. Beat the ingredients together to firm peaks. Divide into 2 equal portions to frost the center and top of the cake. Drizzle the cakes with the caramel sauce. Serve with additional caramel sauce on the side.

Maple Vanilla Bean Cake

SERVES 10–12

MAPLE VANILLA BEAN CAKE

1½ cups **butter**

1 cup **white sugar**

¾ cup **brown sugar**

3 **eggs**

1 large or 2 small **vanilla pods** (or about a tbsp of pure vanilla extract)

1½ cups **all-purpose flour**

1½ cups **cake flour**

2 tsp **baking powder**

¾ cup canned **evaporated milk** (undiluted; measure it straight from the can)

¼ cup **dark maple syrup**

MAPLE GLAZE

2 tbsp melted **butter**

3 tbsp **dark maple syrup**

1 cup **icing sugar** (powdered sugar)

This recipe makes me think, "Great Sunday dinner dessert!" It really is a wonderful example of old-fashioned, home-baked deliciousness—the kind you always eagerly anticipate at the end of Sunday dinner. It's the kind of simple, satisfying recipe that never goes out of style.

The recipe was developed from our family's decades old cherry pound-cake recipe, which uses the concentrated richness of evaporated milk to add great depth of flavour to this buttery, sweet cake.

> **tip** > In many of the cake recipes I've developed, I use a combination of all-purpose flour and cake flour. Cake flour produces a very soft cake that can sometimes be too crumbly. All-purpose flour can sometimes produce too dense a cake texture. Combining the two gives a tender texture with good structure. Apply this idea to other cake recipes and you may just be surprised at the difference it makes.

MAPLE VANILLA BEAN CAKE

1. Preheat oven to 350°F. Grease a Bundt pan well and dust it with flour. If you prefer, this can also be baked in 2 small loaf pans (one for you to enjoy and one to share...if you're still feeling generous after tasting this delectable cake).

2. Cream together the butter, white sugar, and brown sugar until light and fluffy, and then add the eggs, one at a time, beating well after each addition until light and fluffy. Add the seeds and pulp from the inside of the vanilla pods (or 1 tbsp pure vanilla extract).

3. Sift together the all-purpose flour, cake flour, and baking powder.

4. Mix together the evaporated milk and dark maple syrup.

5. Fold the dry ingredients into the creamed mixture alternately with the milk and maple syrup mixture. When alternating, always begin and end with the dry ingredients. This helps to create a more stable structure in the batter. As a general rule, I always add the dry ingredients in 3 portions and the liquid in 2 portions.

6. Pour the mixture into the prepared Bundt pan. Bake in the preheated oven for about 50-60 minutes or until a wooden toothpick inserted in the center comes out clean. Let the cake rest in the pan for 10-15 minutes before turning it out onto a wire rack to cool completely. When cool, drizzle the cake with maple glaze.

MAPLE GLAZE

1. Stir together the melted butter and maple syrup. Whisk the mixture into the icing sugar until smooth and pourable but not too thin in consistency. I hate it when the glaze slides off the cake. If you think it's too thick, add a little more maple syrup; if you think it's too thin, add a little more icing sugar until the proper consistency is achieved. Pour over the cooled cake, and let it sit for 30 minutes before serving.

LEMON CAKE

2¾ cups cake flour

3 tsp baking powder

¼ tsp salt

1 cup unsalted butter, room temperature

2 cups sugar

4 eggs, room temperature

2 tsp vanilla extract

zest of 1 large lemon, finely minced

1¼ cups undiluted evaporated milk

CANDIED LEMON PEEL

juice and zest of 2 lemons

¾ cup sugar

¾ cup water

LEMON CURD

6 lightly beaten egg yolks

1 cup sugar

½ cup fresh lemon juice

zest of 1 lemon, finely minced

½ cup butter cut into small pieces

LEMON BUTTERCREAM FROSTING

2 cups butter

8 cups icing sugar (powdered sugar, confectioners' sugar)

2 tsp vanilla extract

3 tbsp lemon juice

zest of 1 lemon, finely minced

about 4-6 tbsp milk

Ultimate Lemon Cake

With five different lemon components to this cake, it's not hard to see why I've dubbed it the ultimate lemon cake. I start with a homemade lemon scratch cake, which gets brushed with some tangy lemon syrup then filled with alternating layers of rich lemon curd and lemon buttercream frosting before being covered in more of the lemon frosting and finally garnished with homemade candied lemon zest. This is the perfect celebration cake for that lemon lover in your life.

LEMON CAKE

1. Preheat the oven to 325°F. Grease and flour two 9-inch cake pans. Sift together the cake flour, baking powder, and salt, and set aside.

2. Cream together the unsalted butter and sugar until fluffy. Then add the eggs, one at a time, beating well after every addition. Next, beat in the vanilla extract. When this is done, fold in the finely minced lemon zest.

3. Gently fold the dry ingredients into the creamed mixture in three equal portions, alternately with the evaporated milk. When adding dry and wet ingredients alternately in any baking recipe, always begin and end with the dry ingredients.

4. Pour the batter evenly into the prepared cake pans. Bake in the preheated oven for about 35-40 minutes or until a toothpick inserted in the center comes out clean. Watch it carefully; you don't want to over bake this cake. As soon as the toothpick comes out clean, remove the cake from the oven and let it rest in the pans for 5 minutes before turning it out onto a wire rack to cool completely.

CANDIED LEMON PEEL

1. Using a very sharp vegetable peeler, remove the outside zest of 2 large lemons in large strips, avoiding the white part of the peel as much as possible. Add the zest to a very small pot along with the lemon juice, sugar, and water and simmer together gently for about 15-20 minutes. Remove zest and let it drain on a wire rack. Reserve about half the syrup to brush on the cake layers. When the zest is cool, cut the candied zest in thin strips with kitchen scissors. You can also toss in some fine white sugar if you like. I often store the zest in fine sugar until needed.

LEMON CURD

1. In a small saucepan, combine the beaten egg yolks, sugar, ½ cup of fresh lemon juice, and the zest of 1 lemon. Cook slowly over medium-low heat for about 10 minutes, stirring constantly until the mixture thickens enough to coat the back of a wooden spoon.

2. Remove from heat and stir in the butter a few pieces at a time until completely smooth. Cover with plastic wrap and chill completely in the fridge.

LEMON BUTTERCREAM FROSTING

1. Using an electric mixer on low, mix the butter and icing sugar together until the butter breaks up and gets evenly dispersed throughout the sugar in small pieces. The mixture will still appear dry at this point. This stage ensures even distribution and prevents butter lumps in your frosting.

2. Add the vanilla extract, 3 tbsp of lemon juice, zest of 1 lemon, and milk. The milk can be adjusted to make a thicker frosting by adding less, or a more spreadable frosting by adding a little more. Use your own judgement here. The lemon juice can be adjusted to your own taste too.

3. When the icing reaches the desired consistency, continue to beat it on high speed for 5 minutes to incorporate more air into the frosting to make it lighter and fluffier.

to construct the cake >

1. Split the two layers of cake horizontally with a sharp serrated knife to create 4 layers. Brush the reserved syrup onto the cut sides of the cake layers.

2. Place the first layer of cake on the cake plate and top with some of the lemon buttercream frosting. Add the next layer, and using a piping bag (or a heavy plastic bag with a ½-inch opening snipped off the corner) pipe a ring of frosting around the perimeter of the cake. Fill the ring with half of the lemon curd. Add the next layer of cake and top with more of the frosting.

3. Add the final layer of cake. At this point, frost the sides of the cake and pipe a border on the top and bottom. Add the second half of the lemon curd to the top of the cake and garnish the top of the cake with pieces of candied lemon zest. I use kitchen scissors to cut ½-inch pieces to decorate the border and then add a small pile of slivered zest to the center of the cake. Chill for several hours or overnight before serving.

I've always been an unrepentant dessert junkie. All my life I would rather eat half the amount on my plate than forgo dessert. Let's face it though, the evidence points to the fact that I obviously eat both!

I came to cooking through my love of baking and not the other way around, which I don't think is the typical path for most people who are adept in the kitchen. I put it down to being a very finicky eater as a kid, when the only motivation for me to eat those despised vegetables on my plate was the promise of a sweet treat at the end. As an adult, I don't have to have that sweet ending to a meal, and when I do, it's a much smaller portion, but I still love putting together flavours and creating luscious desserts. And I've no doubt that the dozens of decadent desserts I've posted on *Rock Recipes* since I started the website have greatly contributed to its success. Nothing else catches the eye like a decadent drool-worthy dessert, and nothing impresses family and friends like the ability to produce a great one.

Dessert

Homemade Caramel Sauce

I use this delicious, homemade caramel sauce to top several of my desert recipes. And while a good caramel sauce requires your full attention, it's definitely worth it.

> **note** > Timing is very important in a good caramel sauce. So always prepare your ingredients in advance and have them at the ready. And be very careful when preparing caramel sauce; when the sugar syrup hits the right stage to add the butter and cream, the temperature will be over 300°F, so it's important to take particular care. This is not a recipe to attempt with little ones hanging around the kitchen.
>
> It's also very important to use a proper-sized pot. Although the recipe only makes about 3 cups, you'll need a 2½ to 3 quart/liter heavy-bottomed saucepan because the sugar syrup will foam up considerably and produce a significant amount of steam when the butter is added and again when the cream is added. A successful caramel sauce is also one that's been given careful attention. With a little practice you will be a caramel ace in no time.

2 cups sugar

4 tbsp water

⅔ cup butter cut in small cubes

1 cup whipping cream

1. Begin by mixing the sugar and water in a large saucepan. I use a large saucepan of about 3 quarts or larger because the sugar foams up when you add the butter and cream, so make sure you have a large enough pot.

2. Boil the sugar and water over medium heat until the mixture begins to turn a light to medium amber colour. The real skill in making caramel sauce does come with experience and knowing the point at which the colour is perfect. Good advice for beginners is that it's better to be a little too light in colour rather than a little too dark since caramel sauce that's too dark can often taste a little burnt. It's very easy to burn this mixture, which can happen very quickly once the proper colour is achieved, so have your butter and cream at the ready.

3. Do not stir the boiling sugar, this can cause it to crystallize. If you find the sugar starts to crystallize, use a pastry brush to brush water around the inside edge of the pot as it boils. You may have to do this several times. Carefully swirling the pan occasionally is also helpful to avoid crystallization of the sugar.

4. When the colour is right, quickly add the butter and stir quickly until the butter is melted. Remove from the heat immediately and pour in the whipping cream, stirring constantly until the sauce is uniformly smooth. Cool completely.

Baked Sour Cream Flan *with* Roasted Honey Peach Compote

SOUR CREAM FLAN

1¼ cups graham cracker crumbs

¼ cup melted butter

2 tbsp sugar

three 8 oz tubs of sour cream (18% milk fat, i.e., "restaurant style" or "extra thick")

1 cup sugar

3 large eggs

3 tsp vanilla extract

ROASTED HONEY PEACH COMPOTE

3 lbs peaches, peeled and chopped into large chunks

¼ cup honey

¼ tsp cinnamon

pinch of salt

juice of ½ lemon

This sour cream custard flan may be the single most often baked and most often guest-requested dessert ever at our house. I'm sure I've made hundreds of them over the last 25 years or so. The slight tangy note of the sour cream is ideal with fresh berries or berry compotes to top this not-too-sweet but still rich and creamy dessert. This is an ideal go-to recipe to make at any time of the year, following the best of each season's fruits and berries or the preserves made from them during the winter months.

Its secret is its elegant simplicity. This is simply a baked custard sitting on a graham-crumb crust, and it couldn't be easier to prepare. The only trick with this recipe is to not over bake. Once the custard sets, it's done, even if the custard wobbles like well-set jelly at the center. The custard will firm as it cools to a creamy perfection. Almost everyone who tries it at our house leaves with the recipe.

SOUR CREAM FLAN

1. Preheat oven to 325°F. Grease a 9-inch springform pan, lining the bottom with parchment paper to make the flan easier to remove from the pan.

2. Mix the graham cracker crumbs, melted butter, and sugar together until well combined. Then press into the bottom of the greased springform pan.

3. For the custard part of this desert, it's important to use full-fat sour cream, or the filling will not set. I use 18% milk fat sour cream that is sometimes sold as "restaurant style" or "extra thick."

tip > When baking anything in a springform pan, like cheese-cakes or my sour cream flan, I like to line the bottom with a sheet of parchment paper before attaching the side ring for an easier release of the dessert when it has cooled. This parchment does not need to be cut in a perfect circle to fit. I just lay a square sheet of parchment over the bottom circle and attach the side ring. I then trim off any excess paper that sticks out of the bottom. The layer of parchment paper also helps to seal the bottom of the spring-form pan and prevent leakage during baking.

4. Whisk the sour cream, sugar, eggs, and vanilla extract together until the sugar is dissolved. Pour onto the prepared graham-crumb crust and bake in the preheated oven for 55-65 minutes.

5. The custard will still be quite jiggly at the center when done and may be just beginning to brown slightly at the edges, although no colour at all is necessary for the flan to be properly baked. Allow the flan to cool to room temperature then refrigerate for at least a couple of hours, preferably longer, before topping with the peach compote and serving.

ROASTED HONEY PEACH COMPOTE

1. Preheat oven to 400°F. Toss all of the ingredients together and spread in a single layer in a glass baking dish. Bake in the preheated oven for 30-40 minutes, tossing every 10-15 minutes. The cooking time will vary depending on the ripeness of the peaches. Just cook them until the liquid in the baking dish reduces and becomes syrupy. Cool completely before serving.

note > I've chosen this roasted peach compote version to feature here because peach season is my favourite time on the yearly produce calendar. That love comes from summer vacationing in southern Ontario when the wonderfully sweet Niagara area peaches are at their peak. Memories of stopping to buy them at roadside stands and the juice running down my chin at the first bite still have me craving them each summer. Roasting the fruit intensifies its natural flavour making this my ultimate peaches and cream dessert.

Sticky Toffee Pudding

This is the best Sticky Toffee Pudding I've ever tried. It borrows some of the best elements from a few different recipes for this iconic British dessert. Sticky Toffee Pudding should be light in texture with a crumb structure that stands up when baked but collapses in the mouth to a dense, sweet, sticky, soft texture. This recipe hits all of those points and also has a perfect toffee sauce that soaks into the rich moist pudding, lending yet another delicious dimension to this tempting dessert.

I bake these in muffin tins, which for me is the perfect serving size for this very rich dessert. These also freeze quite well and can be thawed and reheated in the microwave or oven before serving.

MAKES 18

STICKY TOFFEE PUDDING

8 oz chopped pitted dried dates

1½ cups water

⅓ cup butter

1 cup firmly packed brown sugar

2 tsp vanilla extract

2 extra-large eggs

3 tbsp molasses

2 tbsp golden syrup (or substitute dark corn syrup)

1⅔ cups all-purpose flour

1½ tsp baking powder

1 tsp baking soda

TOFFEE SAUCE

½ cup whipping cream

¼ cup butter

¼ cup firmly packed brown sugar

1 tbsp molasses

2 tbsp golden syrup

2 tsp vanilla extract

STICKY TOFFEE PUDDING

1. Preheat oven to 350°F. Grease and flour an 18-cup muffin pan.

2. In a small saucepan, add the dates and water, bring to a boil, and simmer over low heat for only a couple of minutes. Let this date mixture stand for a few minutes while preparing the rest of the batter.

3. Cream together the butter, brown sugar, and vanilla extract. Then beat in the eggs, one at a time, beating well after each addition. Add in the molasses and golden syrup, and beat well.

4. Sift together the flour and baking powder, and then add these dry ingredients to the creamed mixture in three equal portions, mixing until smooth after each addition.

5. Puree the date mixture in a food processor or blender before mixing in the baking soda. Add this hot mixture immediately to the batter and mix until smooth. Pour batter into the prepared muffin tins and bake for about 18-20 minutes until the center is just firm. Serve warm with Toffee Sauce.

TOFFEE SAUCE

1. Bring all ingredients to a slow rolling boil for about 2 minutes before serving over the baked puddings.

Coconut Cream Pie

Although I love coconut cream pie, I never order it in restaurants because of decades of being served gelatinous slop that bears little resemblance to the real thing. I have been making this pie since I was 12 years old and have yet to sample better than this decades old recipe.

SERVES 10–12

PIE CRUST (MAKES SUFFICIENT PASTRY FOR TWO 10-INCH PIE SHELLS)

1 cup **very cold butter** cut into small cubes

2½ cups flour

½ tsp salt

¼ to ⅓ cup ice water (only enough to make a dough form)

COCONUT CREAM FILLING

3 cups whole milk

⅓ cup flour

⅔ cup sugar

pinch of salt

1 cup unsweetened fine dried coconut

3 slightly beaten extra-large egg yolks

4 tbsp butter

2 tsp vanilla extract

¼ tsp pure almond extract

VANILLA WHIPPED CREAM

1 cup whipping cream

1 tsp vanilla extract

3 tbsp icing sugar

tip > A good flaky pie pastry depends on very cold ingredients, including the butter and water. Some people even put the flour for their pastry in the freezer before using it. Using as little water to bind the dough as possible and working the dough as little as possible are also crucial to good pastry. Resting the dough for at least 20 minutes in the fridge before rolling is very important, as is a fully preheated oven. Going straight from cold to hot is beneficial for most pastries, so chilling the prepared pie crust in the pie plate before it goes in the oven is also a good habit to cultivate.

PIE CRUST

1. Using a food processor or a pastry blender, cut cold butter into the flour and salt until the mixture resembles a coarse meal. Small pea-sized pieces of butter should still be visible. Pour the cold water over the mixture and work in by tossing with a fork until a dough begins to form. Use your hands as little as possible and work the dough as little as possible. I like to sort of press the pastry together into balls with a minimum of kneading. Divide the dough into 2 balls, flatten into 1½-inch thick rounds, wrap in plastic wrap and place in the refrigerator to rest for a minimum of 20 minutes. You can freeze the second round to use another time.

2. You can make your dough the previous day, but make sure you take it out of the fridge for 10-20 minutes to warm slightly before rolling out.

3. Roll the dough into a 12-inch round and place in the bottom of a 10-inch pie plate. Trim and flute the edges as desired. Poke a few holes in the bottom of the pastry shell with a fork, especially in the corners, and rest the pie shell in the refrigerator for an additional 10-20 minutes before baking at 400°F for 12-15 minutes or until golden brown. Cool completely before adding the filling.

COCONUT CREAM FILLING

1. Scald the whole milk in the microwave or on the stove top to very hot but not boiling. A microwave works best as there is no chance of burning the milk.

2. Meanwhile, in a saucepan, combine the flour, sugar, salt, and dried coconut. Over medium-low flame slowly add 1 cup of the scalded milk, whisking constantly. As you notice the filling beginning to thicken, add another cup of the scalded milk, continuing to stir constantly until it begins to thicken again. Add the final cup of scalded milk, stirring constantly. Continue to cook over medium-low heat until mixture begins to slightly thicken.

3. At this point, remove the filling from heat and pour about ½ cup of this mixture onto the egg yolks, whisking constantly. Pour the egg mixture immediately back into the pot, continuing to constantly stir. Cook for an additional 2-3 minutes until the filling reaches pudding consistency and then remove from the flame. The mixture should just be beginning to boil at this point.

4. Stir in the butter, vanilla extract, and almond extract. Cool almost to room temperature before pouring into the baked pie shell. Chill for about 3 hours or even overnight.

VANILLA WHIPPED CREAM

1. Combine all ingredients and beat to soft peaks then spread on top of the cooled coconut cream filling. Garnish with toasted coconut and serve.

Chocolate Orange Cheesecake

I developed this recipe about 15 years ago around the holidays when Santa, in his regular generosity, inspired me by leaving that familiar favourite, a Terry's Chocolate Orange, in the toe of my Christmas stocking. Since then, this recipe has proven to be the most popular of the many cheesecakes in my repertoire. Probably because of the great popularity of Terry's Chocolate Orange in the UK, the Brits, who have sampled this cheesecake, have gone mad for it. It has made many repeat appearances and has become a bit of a tradition at my annual family Christmas feast too.

SERVES 12–16

CHOCOLATE ORANGE CHEESECAKE

1½ cups Oreo Cookie Crumbs

⅓ cup melted butter

3 tbsp sugar

1½ lbs cream cheese

1¼ cups sugar

3 large eggs

2 tsp vanilla extract

¾ cup whipping cream

1½ squares unsweetened baking chocolate, melted (in a pinch, substitute ½ cup cocoa, but add another ¼ cup whipping cream)

zest of 2 medium or 1 large orange, finely minced

GANACHE GLAZE

¼ cup whipping cream

¾ cup semisweet or dark chocolate chips

note > A word about baking a cheesecake in a bain-marie before starting the recipe. A bain-marie is simply a water bath that buffers the direct heat from the sides and bottom of the baking pan to more evenly bake the cheesecake from the sides to the center.

I bake my cheesecakes in a 9-inch or 10-inch springform pan that has the bottom and sides wrapped in 2 or 3 layers of wide, heavy-duty aluminum foil, which forms a sort of boat that the cheesecake pan sits in to make sure no water leaks in to ruin the crust of my cheesecake. The aluminum foil wrapped pan is then placed inside a larger baking pan; I use a 12-inch cake pan. Boiling water is then poured into the larger pan, filling it from ½ to ⅔ of the way to the top. I find it best to pour the boiling water into the pan after it's placed on the rack in the oven as you are less likely to splash water onto the cheesecake or inside the aluminum foil.

Even if you choose not to use the water bath, wrapping the pan in aluminum foil is still a good idea because it will act as a partial heat buffer, making the cheesecake bake more evenly.

CHOCOLATE ORANGE CHEESECAKE

1. Preheat oven to 300°F. Grease the bottom but not the sides of a 9-inch or 10-inch springform pan and line the bottom with parchment paper.

2. Mix together the Oreo Cookie Crumbs, melted butter, and 3 tbsp sugar, and press into the pan.

3. Cream together the cream cheese and 1¼ cups sugar. Add the eggs, one at a time, beating well after each addition. Then add the vanilla extract and whipping cream. Blend until smooth and divide mixture into 2 equal portions.

4. To the first half of the mixture, stir in the melted baking chocolate, pour into the bottom of the prepared springform pan.

5. To the second half of the mixture, stir in the orange zest. Carefully spoon this mixture over the top of the chocolate mixture already in the pan.

6. Bake in the preheated oven for about 60-70 minutes or until the surface of the cake no longer looks glossy. Remove from oven and immediately run a sharp knife around the edge of the pan to prevent cracking. Cool completely in the pan. Top with chocolate ganache glaze.

GANACHE GLAZE

1. In a heavy bottomed pot, scald but do not boil the whipping cream. Then add the chocolate chips and melt on low heat.

2. Pour over the cooled cake, or to create ganache lace: cool slightly and spoon into a piping bag fitted with a number 3 tip (a heavy Ziploc bag with the corner snipped of works just as well). Pipe over the entire cake in a circular, overlapping, swirling pattern, repeating coverage all over the cake until all ganache glaze is used. Garnish with orange segments, orange zest curls, or orange slices.

Raspberry Buttercream Mille-Feuille

What I love about this version of the classic French pastry is that it looks impressive but is actually not difficult to make. In French, mille-feuille literally translated means *a thousand leaves* and is named for the many layers in the puff pastry upon which it's based. Traditionally, the layers are filled with pastry cream, but I decided to fill them with some easy vanilla buttercream frosting and raspberry jam to make them easier to serve and more portable, even as an addition to a summer picnic basket.

PUFF PASTRIES

1 lb package frozen puff pastry

VANILLA BUTTERCREAM FROSTING

4 cups icing sugar (powdered sugar)

1 cup butter

2 tsp vanilla extract

a few tbsp milk

good quality raspberry jam

VANILLA GLAZE

1½ cups icing sugar (powdered sugar)

1 tsp vanilla extract

milk

¼ cup chocolate chips

1 tsp butter

> **tip** > This recipe makes 8 pastries, but these are quite rich, so I most often cut 16 squares out of them and serve at that size.

PUFF PASTRIES

1. Preheat oven to 425°F.

2. Roll out the puff pastry into three 8-inch squares. Place on a parchment-lined cookie sheet. You may have to bake these one at a time depending on the size of your cookie sheet. Dock the pastry by poking holes in it with a fork about every ½ inch over the entire surface of the pastry. Chill it in the freezer for 10 minutes to ensure it is well chilled. Puff pastry must be baked very cold. Place another sheet of parchment paper on top of the pastry and weigh it down with another cookie sheet on top. This keeps the pastry from puffing too much and ensures it's crispy when baked.

3. Bake in the preheated oven for about 15 minutes. Then decrease the heat to 375°F, remove the top pan and top sheet of parchment paper, and bake for about another 5 minutes or so until it's evenly medium golden brown throughout. Cool the baked pastry sheets completely before filling.

VANILLA BUTTERCREAM FROSTING

1. Blend the icing sugar, butter, vanilla extract, and milk together until smooth. Only add a little milk at the beginning, and then add more if you need it. You want a very thick frosting here. It should still be easily spreadable, but as thick as possible is best.

2. Take ¼ of the frosting and spread it evenly on 1 layer of the baked pastry. On top of the frosting, spread a thin layer of very good quality raspberry jam.

3. Spread another ¼ of the frosting onto the next sheet of baked pastry and invert it on top of the raspberry jam so the jam is sandwiched between 2 thin layers of frosting. This technique helps the completed pastry hold together better.

4. Next, spread another ¼ of the frosting onto the top of the inverted pastry layer, followed by another thin layer of raspberry jam. Finally spread the last of the frosting onto the last sheet of baked puff pastry and invert that onto the raspberry jam. Chill the constructed mille-feuille while you prepare the glaze for the top.

VANILLA GLAZE

1. Blend together the icing sugar, vanilla extract, and milk well, using only enough milk to bring the glaze to a very thick consistency. The glaze should be just at the point where it almost isn't pourable but still goes to a flat surface when you stop stirring, even if it takes a couple of seconds to do so. Spread the glaze evenly over the surface of the constructed mille-feuille.

2. Melt together the chocolate chips and butter. Then spoon the melted chocolate into a Ziploc bag and snip the corner off with scissors. The opening should be quite small, about the size of a pencil lead. Draw lines of chocolate all across the surface of the glaze, parallel to each other and about a ½ inch apart. Using the back of a knife or a toothpick, draw lines perpendicular to the chocolate lines across the surface of the glaze, about every inch, alternating the direction of the lines as you go.

3. Chill the completed mille-feuille for at least a couple of hours, preferably longer. Trim all four edges of the pastry so you have straight sides before cutting into 8 rectangles or 16 squares. The trimmings are the bakers bonus...enjoy!

Banoffee Pie

Those who know me well will tell you I'm very fond of British television, in particular their excellent selection of cooking programs. Although more an entertainment program than a cooking show, *Come Dine with Me* features several contestants who each throw a dinner party on successive evenings and are then rated on their food and hosting skills by their competitors. There's a Canadian version now as well. The British version is where I was first introduced to Banoffee Pie. It must be the most served dessert course ever on the show.

When I decided to enter a dessert recipe for the Home Chef Challenge on NBC's *Today Show* website, it was the perfect opportunity to develop my own version of the UK favourite. With great support from *Rock Recipes* followers, I'm pleased to report it won the online competition, beating out the other two contenders with 70% of the public vote. Since then, this pie has become one of the most popular desserts ever on *Rock Recipes*.

BISCUIT BASE

2¼ cups digestive biscuit crumbs or graham cracker crumbs

½ cup melted butter

3 tbsp sugar

TOFFEE FILLING

½ cup melted butter

½ cup firmly packed brown sugar

2 tsp vanilla extract

one 10 oz (300 ml) can sweetened condensed milk

BANANA CREAM TOPPING

2 cups whipping cream

3 tbsp icing sugar

1 tsp vanilla extract

4 ripe bananas, sliced

BISCUIT BASE

1. Preheat oven to 350°F.

2. Pulse digestive biscuits in a food processor then mix together the crumbs, melted butter, and sugar. Press into the bottom and sides of a lightly greased 9-inch springform pan, about 1½ inch up the sides of the pan will do.

3. Bake in the preheated oven for 10-12 minutes. Remove from oven and cool in the pan on a wire rack.

TOFFEE FILLING

1. In a small saucepan, combine the melted butter, brown sugar, and vanilla extract. Bring to a slow boil until foamy, and then add the sweetened condensed milk.

2. Bring back to a slow boil over medium-low heat and cook, stirring continuously for another 5-10 minutes until the mixture darkens slightly. You can use a candy thermometer to bring the mixture to soft ball stage of about 235°F if you want to be exact. Remove from heat and pour into the prepared biscuit base. Chill for 2 hours or more until thoroughly cooled.

BANANA CREAM TOPPING

1. Add the whipping cream, icing sugar, and vanilla extract to the bowl of an electric mixer and beat together until soft peaks form. Then gently fold in the sliced bananas.

2. Spread the Banana Cream Topping over the toffee filling, and garnish the top of the pie with chocolate shavings if desired. Chill for about another hour before serving.

S'mores Tart

This recipe was inspired by a deeper dish S'mores Pie I once made. I loved the look of the pie with its golden toasted marshmallow top, but the ganache filling was a bit thick and dense for my taste. So I decided to try a much shallower version in an 11-inch fluted-edge tart pan using a chocolate tart filling. Another reason I opted for the larger, shallower pan was to fit more marshmallows on the top for a better marshmallow to chocolate ratio. If you don't have a large tart pan, use your largest pie plate and add a few minutes to the baking time.

Though this recipe's bound to be popular with kids, I think it's elegant enough to serve at any dinner party and sure to be enjoyed by the young and young at heart. After all, who doesn't love s'mores?

GRAHAM CRUMB CRUST

2 cups graham cracker crumbs

⅓ cup + 1 tbsp melted butter

2 tbsp sugar

FILLING

7 oz whipping cream

3 oz milk

7 oz (by weight) dark chocolate, chopped into small pieces

1 large beaten egg

1 tsp vanilla

one ½ lb (250 g) bag large marshmallows

GRAHAM CRUMB CRUST

1. Lightly grease an 11-inch tart pan.

2. Mix together the graham cracker crumbs, melted butter, and sugar, and then press into the bottom and sides of the greased tart pan.

FILLING

1. Preheat oven to 350°F.

2. Bring the cream and milk just to boiling and pour the hot liquid over the chopped chocolate. Let stand for 5 minutes, and then whisk together until smooth. Cool for about 10 minutes before whisking in the beaten egg and vanilla.

3. Pour into the prepared crust and bake for about 20 minutes. The center can still be a little wobbly at this point. The surface should still be shiny.

4. Remove from oven, change the oven setting to broil, and move the oven rack to the bottom. Place the tart on a pizza pan or large circular baking pan. This will later allow you to easily turn the tart as the marshmallows toast.

5. Cut the marshmallows in half with kitchen scissors and start by placing one marshmallow half in the center of the tart, arrange the rest of the marshmallow pieces in a tight circular pattern right to the edge of the crust.

6. Place in the oven under the broiler and, watching closely, broil until the top is evenly golden brown. I like to rotate the pan about every 15 seconds to ensure even browning. The entire process should take just a few minutes.

7. Cool the tart to room temperature before serving. If refrigerating the tart, for best results, allow it to come back up to room temperature before serving. Serve with a drizzle of chocolate ganache if desired.

Prince William's Chocolate Biscuit Cake

I went for a stroll downtown with the kids just around the time of William and Kate's royal wedding, and we came up with the idea to make Prince William's groom's cake, which he'd specially requested be served at the reception. Apparently, this easy, no-bake refrigerator cake is a childhood indulgence of his and according to a former Buckingham Palace chef, a particular favourite of the entire royal family. With this idea in mind, we dropped into Fat Nanny's grocery store on Duckworth Street, where I procured the necessary Lyle's golden syrup and a large sleeve of McVities original digestive biscuits. Both Lyle's and McVities are venerable brands in the UK, which adds a little extra British authenticity to the recipe.

Golden syrup is a little difficult to come by in these parts, so I'd use dark corn syrup as a substitute, and of course, any brand of digestive biscuits will do. Dark chocolate is the way to go with this recipe, but you can mix semisweet and dark chocolate if you like the chocolate flavour to be a little lighter. I've also read numerous versions of this recipe that include such ingredients as dried cherries, roasted nuts, and one ingredient I might just try the next time I make this...broken honeycomb toffee bars! There's lots of room for experimentation with this recipe, so go discover your own favourite version.

SERVES 20

PRINCE WILLIAM'S CHOCOLATE BISCUIT CAKE

1 lb unsalted butter

2 lbs dark chocolate, roughly chopped (about 50% cocoa)

pinch of salt

¼ cup whipping cream

⅓ cup golden syrup

1 lb digestive biscuits, broken by hand into postage stamp-sized pieces (vanilla wafers or oat cookies make a good substitute)

CHOCOLATE GANACHE

½ cup whipping cream

8 oz dark chocolate, chopped

1 tbsp corn syrup

tip > Another serving suggestion would be to make half the recipe and use a 9x9 parchment paper-lined baking dish. This will allow you to cut the dessert into small squares or bars to serve.

PRINCE WILLIAM'S CHOCOLATE BISCUIT CAKE

1. Melt the butter over medium-low heat. Add the chocolate and salt and continue over medium-low heat until the chocolate is fully melted. Remove from heat and stir in the whipping cream and golden syrup until smooth.

2. Fold in the broken biscuits and pour into a 9-inch springform pan lined with plastic wrap or parchment paper.

3. Chill in the fridge for at least 3 hours or overnight. Remove from pan and glaze with chocolate ganache.